# THE AFFAIR

*A Play*

# THE AFFAIR

*A Play*

BY RONALD MILLAR

*from the novel*

BY C. P. SNOW

*NEW YORK*

CHARLES SCRIBNER'S SONS

August, 1963

The *Affair* was first presented in the U.S. by Bonard Productions and Henry Sherek at Henry Miller's Theatre, New York City, N.Y., on September 20, 1962, with the following cast:

## CAST

(In order of appearance)

| | |
|---|---|
| THOMAS CRAWFORD, SC.D., F.R.S., *Master* | KYNASTON REEVES |
| TOM ORBELL, M.A., *Lecturer in History* | CHRISTOPHER HEWETT |
| CLUB STEWARD | MITCHELL ERICKSON |
| SIR LEWIS ELIOT, K.B.E., M.A. | BREWSTER MASON |
| LAURA HOWARD | BRENDA VACCARO |
| MARTIN ELIOT, PH.D., *Lecturer in Physics* | KENNETH MARS |
| G. H. WINSLOW, M.A. | FRANCIS COMPTON |
| LESTER INCE, M.A., F.B.A., HON. LITT.D., *Senior Fellow* | |
| | EDWARD ATIENZA |
| JULIAN SKEFFINGTON, SC.D., *Demonstrator in Physics* | |
| | DONALD MOFFAT |
| ARTHUR BROWN, M.A., *Senior Tutor* | EDGAR DANIELS |
| SIR FRANCIS GETLIFFE, C.B.E., SC.D., F.R.S., *Professor of Physics* | |
| | GEOFFREY LUMSDEN |
| ALEX NIGHTINGALE, SC.D., *Bursar* | PATRICK WADDINGTON |
| MARGARET ELIOT | ELIZABETH HUBBARD |
| DONALD HOWARD, PH.D. | KEITH BAXTER |
| NEWBY, THE COLLEGE PORTER | C. STAFFORD DICKENS |
| GILBERT DAWSON-HILL, M.A., Q.C. | PAXTON WHITEHEAD |

*Directed by John Fernald*

*Settings and Lighting by Eldon Elder*

*Costumes by Ramse Mostoller with Brewster Mason*

# SYNOPSIS OF SCENES

*Prologue*    CAMBRIDGE

## ACT ONE

*Scene 1* A CORNER OF A LONDON CLUB

*Scene 2* THE COMBINATION ROOM OF A CAMBRIDGE COLLEGE

*Scene 3* LEWIS ELIOT'S FLAT IN LONDON

## ACT TWO

*Scene 1* MARTIN ELIOT'S ROOMS IN COLLEGE

*Scene 2* A BED-ROOM IN ROMSEY TOWN, CAMBRIDGE

*Scene 3* THE COMBINATION ROOM

## ACT THREE

THE COMBINATION ROOM

*(During this act, the lights will be lowered to denote the passage of several hours)*

# ACT ONE

# ACT ONE

*Prologue*

*The houselights fade and the College bells toll in the darkness.
The curtain rises on a darkened stage—then a single light fades
in on the Master of the College,* THOMAS CRAWFORD, *standing
centre stage as the bells die away in the distance. Behind him
are the heraldic arms of the College. In his hand* CRAWFORD *holds
a copy of the Order of Deprivation of Donald Howard.* CRAW-
FORD *is a distinguished, Buddha-faced man of seventy-three. He
wears the red robes of his office.*

CRAWFORD

We come now to the final stage in these proceedings—the finding
of the Court of Seniors. That finding is unanimous.

Speaking as both Master of the College and President of the Court,
I am bound to say that in formulating that finding I have never en-
countered a more painful duty.

*(He puts on his spectacles and reads:)*

"October 17th, 1959. At a meeting of the Court of Seniors held this
day, present, the Master, Mr. Winslow, Mr. Brown, Dr. Nightingale,
it was resolved as follows: That having heard the evidence relating
to the thesis and publications of Dr. D. C. Howard, Fellow of this
College, the Court orders that Dr. Howard be deprived of that Fellowship forthwith, the deprivation to date from this day, that pay-
ment of dividends and commons allowance to Dr. Howard cease
forthwith, that Dr. Howard be no longer regarded as a member of

the Fellowship of this College, and that he be deemed to have forfeited all rights and privileges that pertain thereto."

The Order is signed by the four members of the Court and sealed with the College Seal.

(*The light fades out and the Curtain rises on—*)

# ACT ONE

*Scene 1*

A CORNER OF A LONDON CLUB. EVENING

TOM

Thank you, Roberts.

> TOM ORBELL, *a large young man in his late twenties, smooth, fleshy and affable, is seated comfortably in an armchair, leafing idly through a glossy magazine. A* CLUB STEWARD *is serving him with a drink.*

STEWARD

Thank you, sir. Will you be dining tonight, sir?

TOM

Yes, I have a guest table. There'll be three of us.

STEWARD

Very good, sir.

> (*He turns to go.*)

TOM

Roberts, when Sir Lewis Eliot arrives, tell him I'm in here, would you?

STEWARD

Yes, sir.

> (*As he is about to go out, he stops.*)

Sir Lewis is just coming in now, sir.

TOM

Oh. Right.

(*The* STEWARD *goes out.*)

STEWARD

(*Off*)

Good evening, Sir Lewis.

LEWIS

(*Off*)

Good evening, Roberts.

STEWARD

(*Off*)

Mr. Orbell is waiting in the smoking room, sir.

LEWIS

(*Off*)

Good. Thank you.

(LEWIS ELIOT *enters. At a glance,* LEWIS *might be many things —a don, a barrister—both of which he has been—a senior civil servant—which he now is. Sharp-eyed, watchful, with a humorous mouth,* LEWIS *is forty-eight.*)

Hello, Tom. Am I late?

TOM

(*Rising effusively*)

Lewis! My dear Lewis! How are you?

LEWIS

I'm well. And you?

TOM

Putting on weight where I shouldn't, dammit. There must be a way of keeping it down.

**LEWIS**

There is. Eat less.

**TOM**

I know, I know. I overdo the fleshpots—love every second of it. Let's have a drink, shall we?

**LEWIS**

(*Sitting*)

Well, how's Cambridge?

**TOM**

Same as ever. Chapel bells—weeping willows—and, underneath the Rupert Brooke, dog eat dog. Or, rather, don eat don.

**LEWIS**

(*Amused*)

Who's eating you?

**TOM**

No one—at the moment, I'm indigestible.

**LEWIS**

I thought I detected a bitter note.

**TOM**

Heavens, no. I worship the place. But I've no illusions about it. I know what's what.

**LEWIS**

Yes, dear Tom, you always have.

**TOM**

Well, in the academic jungle, you've got to watch your step, haven't you?

(*With a touch of nervousness*)

By the way, Lewis, I—er—I've asked someone to join us tonight. Is that all right?

**LEWIS**

Of course. Do I know him?

**TOM**

It's a woman. My dear Lewis, she really is rather striking.

**LEWIS**

My dear Tom, I'm sure she is.

**TOM**

No, it's nothing like that. Between you and me it's a bit of a chore. That's really why I asked you to come along.

**LEWIS**

Oh! What am I supposed to do?

**TOM**

I'm not asking you to *do* anything. Just be here. I mean, she can't very well bring it up in front of you.

**LEWIS**

Bring what up?

**TOM**

The poor girl's got a bee in her bonnet, about—I'm not sure if I ought to tell you.

**LEWIS**

Then don't.

**TOM**

You won't repeat it?

**LEWIS**

I won't repeat it.

(*Pause*)

**TOM**

This may come as rather a shock, but a few months ago the College narrowly avoided a public scandal.

LEWIS
You mean the Howard affair?

TOM

(*Surprised*)

You heard?

LEWIS
A whisper, nothing more.

TOM
Who from—Martin?

LEWIS
And Francis Getliffe, last time I was up.

TOM
It's all supposed to be intramural—not a word outside the College.

LEWIS
I rather think that as an ex-Fellow they counted me academically an insider.

TOM
My dear Lewis, of course. The fact is, for some reason best known to herself, Howard's wife, Laura, has got it into her head that I sympathise with her husband.

LEWIS
And do you?

TOM
I can't stand the sight of the man. Nor can anyone else that I ever met. Except of course, Laura, and God knows what she sees. However—she's persuaded herself that Donald's been victimised by the College.

LEWIS
And has he?

TOM
No, it's all damned nonsense. But she sees the whole thing as a sort of Dreyfus affair, with Howard as Dreyfus.

LEWIS
And how does she see you? As Zola?

TOM
If she does, she's punting up the wrong river. Howard's done for, and good riddance, but you can't tell a woman to her face that you're delighted her husband's got the boot. I wish she'd stay away from me.

(*The* HALL PORTER *has entered.*)

PORTER
Mrs. Howard, sir.

(LAURA HOWARD *comes in. A dark, determined, handsome woman, about thirty.*)

TOM
My dear Laura, how very nice! Do you know Sir Lewis Eliot?

LAURA
No, I don't.

(*The* PORTER *goes out.*)

TOM
Martin's brother.

LEWIS
How do you do?

LAURA
How do you do?

TOM

Lewis is dining with us tonight.

LAURA

(*Taken aback*)

Oh!

TOM

Yes, I ran into him quite by accident and I knew you wouldn't mind if he joined us. Now sit down, my dear. You take the place of honour.

(LAURA *sits in the centre chair.*)

Lewis was a Fellow before the war, but he went and left us. Cambridge is like everywhere else in this country. Everything's got into the hands of the awful old men, and when someone like Lewis comes along, who might conceivably do something about it, off he goes to Whitehall or someplace and leaves the old men to sit on the heads of the rest of us. The College misses him very much.

LAURA

I'm sure it does.

(*The* STEWARD *appears.*)

TOM

Now, what will you have?

LAURA

Nothing, thank you.

TOM

Oh, come.

LAURA

A small dry sherry.

TOM

Lewis?

LEWIS

Gin and tonic.

TOM

(*To* STEWARD)

Large.

STEWARD

Very good, sir.

(*He exits.*)

TOM

(*Offering cigarettes*)

Yes, ever since the confounded war the good young middle-aged, like Lewis, have got caught up trying to keep the country afloat. That leaves it to the rest of us—the generation coming up—to smash the awful old men. We're all in it together. We're going to show them. I mean it very sincerely, both of you.

LAURA

(*Abruptly*)

What are you going to do about Donald?

TOM

(*Taken aback*)

I'm afraid there's nothing we *can* do tonight.

LAURA

We can plan. What are your plans?

TOM

(*Defensive*)

I can't do anything by myself, can I?

LAURA

Why can't you?

TOM

Do you seriously believe that the Court of Seniors is going to listen to a solitary Junior Fellow? I'm speaking with great affection for you, my dear—and for Donald, of course. You've got to be very careful about your tactics. And, incidentally, so have I. I'm still part of the College.

LAURA

You're lucky.

TOM

Oh, I don't know. After all, what's a Fellowship? Six years academic glory with no guarantee of renewal. They'll probably kick me out, too, when my time's up.

LAURA

Donald's time was *not* up.

TOM

No, and don't think I don't sympathise. It's a damn shame, but, you know, he'll probably be a whole lot better off with I.C.I. or something.

LAURA

Even supposing it appealed to him, "I.C.I. or something" is not open to him—after what happened.

(*The* STEWARD *returns with the drinks.*)

TOM

Ah! Roberts.

(STEWARD *places the sherry in front of* LAURA *and the gin and tonic in front of* LEWIS.)

LEWIS

Thank you, Roberts.

STEWARD

Thank you, sir.

(*He exits.*)

TOM

(*To* LAURA, *raising his glass*)

To you, my dear.

LAURA

To justice.

TOM

Yes, of course.

(*They drink.*)

I say, that's a charming brooch. I haven't seen that before, have I?

LAURA

So you have no plans.

TOM

Now, I didn't say that. But I do feel very sincerely that you ought to consider this affair from every angle before you start something. Lewis agrees with me, don't you, Lewis?

LAURA

(*Turning to* LEWIS)

How much do *you* know about this business?

LEWIS

Only that a few months ago the College dismissed one of its younger science Fellows.

LAURA

Do you know why they dismissed him?

LEWIS

I gathered it was something to do with his work.

LAURA

(*Hard*)

My husband was brought before the Court of Seniors and charged
with scientific fraud. Charged, convicted, disgraced, dismissed. They
ruined him. Did you gather that?

LEWIS

I heard only the barest outline.

LAURA

(*With passion*)

Did you hear that it's a piece of unforgivable injustice?

LEWIS

No.

LAURA

Did you hear that it's the result of sheer, blind political prejudice?

TOM

My dear Laura, with great respect, you're misleading yourself. Of
course most of the College doesn't agree with Donald's political
views. I don't myself, as you know very well. But then I don't agree
with Lewis's politics either, and I think that Lewis would feel pretty
safe in his job if I suddenly became part of the Establishment. Speaking with great affection, you're on the wrong track.

LAURA

I don't believe it for an instant.

TOM

I give you my word—

LAURA

I'll believe you when you've done something to prove it.

TOM

I've told you, I can't.

LAURA

You mean you won't.

TOM

My dear, I simply don't have the power.

LAURA

You don't have the guts.

TOM

That's not true.

LAURA

Look, I'm not asking you anything difficult. All I want is to get the case re-opened.

TOM

You don't seem to understand. You're dealing with a society, with a constitution. I'm just one out of twenty, a very junior person. I'm not a majority of the College. You need a majority of the College before the thing can be so much as raised again. That's true, Lewis, isn't it?

LEWIS

Yes, Mrs. Howard, I'm afraid it is.

LAURA

We'll never get a majority of the College unless someone, some-where, makes a beginning. I'm asking you to begin. Well?

TOM

Let's go in and dine, shall we? And then over some really excellent turtle soup, I'll explain my position.

LAURA

No, I think I'll go.

TOM

Laura!

LAURA

I understand your position perfectly. There's nothing to explain.

TOM

Now look, my dear. Let's be practical. I can't make any impact on this situation at all. Frankly, it's just not on. But wait! Here's a suggestion. Why not try to persuade Lewis here to take a hand?

LEWIS

Now wait a minute, Tom—

TOM

(*Smoothly, unabashed*)

His brother Martin is Junior Tutor. Most of the others are former colleagues. As one of the biggest legal wigs in Whitehall, he's our nearest approach to an Elder Statesman, is Lewis. He can talk to the awful old men, as I can't possibly and shan't be able to for another twenty years.

LEWIS

I think you'll manage.

TOM

No, I mean it, very sincerely. It's the legal mind *you* want. Lewis is the man for you.

LAURA

(*To* LEWIS)

Are you in touch with them nowadays?

LEWIS

Not really, no.

LAURA
What could you do?

LEWIS
Probably nothing.

TOM
Don't you believe it. Surely, Lewis, you'll be up for the Audit feast?

LEWIS
Yes, I shall, but that is a social occasion and I shall be a guest.

TOM
I know, I know. But couldn't you put out one or two feelers or something?

(*Pause*)

LEWIS

(*At length*)

Mrs. Howard, I shall be in Cambridge for Christmas. If it would be of any help, I will put out one or two feelers—have a word with my brother—

TOM
You see? You see? Action already.

LEWIS
Without prejudice, of course.

TOM
Naturally Lewis couldn't commit himself to an opinion, one way or the other. Any more than I could commit myself, could I?

LAURA

(*Quietly*)

No. No, you couldn't commit yourselves.

(*Big Ben is heard striking in the distance.*)

TOM

(*Comfortably*)

Then that's settled. Lewis will put out feelers. I say, it was a bit of luck bumping into old Lewis like that, wasn't it? And now, my dear, shall we go in?

(*He takes her arm and leads her toward the dining-room.*)

They tell me we have grouse on the menu tonight and the chicken livers really are rather delicious—it's a speciality of the club. . . .

*THE CURTAIN IS DOWN.*

(*The chimes of Big Ben change to the bells of Cambridge.*)

*THE CURTAIN RISES ON —*

## ACT ONE

*Scene 2*

THE COMBINATION ROOM OF A CAMBRIDGE COLLEGE. CHRISTMAS EVE

*Four comfortable chairs are spread out in a broad crescent facing the fire, which is in the fourth wall. The glow of the fire illuminates the faces of the occupants. In addition to* LEWIS ELIOT, *there are five Fellows of the College—*WINSLOW, GAY, TOM ORBELL, INCE *and* MARTIN ELIOT. WINSLOW *is eighty,* GAY *is ninety-four,* MARTIN *just under forty, and* INCE *thirty.* PROFESSOR GAY *is asleep, with his gown round his shoulders like a shawl. Other gowns are strewn around the room. Behind the chairs, a long rosewood table is set out with the after-dinner wine which they are taking.* TOM ORBELL *is seated at the table peeling an apple.* WINSLOW *is eating nuts.* INCE *is dispensing the port.*

MARTIN

Oh, come, Winslow, wasn't there a time when *you* wanted to be Master?

WINSLOW

Never, my dear Tutor, never. As a former Bursar, I already have my niche in history. I was the worst since the College was founded four hundred years ago.

(INCE *puts the decanter down on the table by* WINSLOW, *having poured him a glass.*)

Ah, I believe this bottle is being presented by Mr. Eliot, for the purpose—correct me if I'm wrong, my dear Tutor—of marking the reappearance here of his brother.

28

MARTIN
Yes, I thought it was a good idea.

WINSLOW
A remarkable display of fraternal good wishes. Gentlemen, the Eliots
—Lewis and Martin!

(*The toast is drunk. The* ELIOTS *murmur their thanks.*)

WINSLOW
And how long are you in Cambridge, my dear Eliot?

LEWIS
Just for the holiday.

MARTIN
Or until our respective children come to blows. At the moment
there's comparative peace.

LEWIS
The afterglow of carols in Chapel. It won't last.

INCE
(*Who has enjoyed his wine*)
Chapel? Well now, isn't that nice?

(*To* SKEFFINGTON, *who has just entered*)
And how about you, Skeffington, old son? How do you propose to
celebrate the Nativity? Midnight Mass with all the trimmings?

SKEFFINGTON
Certainly.

INCE
Stone the crows.

SKEFFINGTON

It happens to be a religious festival. That's the way to do it, you know.

(*He removes his gown and throws it on a chair.* SKEFFINGTON *is thirty-nine.*)

INCE

It's not my way, old darling. I shall do my stuff with wife and kid-dies, bless their demanding little hearts. I shall then retire with said wife, three bottles of the cheapest vino on the market, and the old jazz-box. We shall then proceed to get gently sozzled to the strains of Humphrey Lyttleton and other splendid noises. In view of which pending debauch, this little piggy is off to bye-byes. Nighty-night to one and all.

(*He sees the sleeping* GAY *and drops a kiss on the top of his head.*)

Night, night.

(*He exits.*)

WINSLOW

In what does that young man instruct the younger generation?

MARTIN

The music of Bach, Beethoven and Brahms.

WINSLOW

Remarkable. It cannot too often be said that, with a modicum of ex-ceptions, Cambridge dons are not distinguished men. They are just men who confer distinctions upon one another.

LEWIS

(*Softly*)

And occasionally, having conferred them, remove them.

WINSLOW

I'm not entirely sure that I follow our guest.

LEWIS

I was thinking of Donald Howard.

(*A sudden silence*)

WINSLOW

(*At length*)

Hardly a profitable thought, I fear, even in the spuriously charitable context of Christmas.

TOM

Which service are *you* attending tomorrow, Winslow?

WINSLOW

My dear young man, you should know by now that I don't support these primitive survivals. Since I was elected a Fellow of this College, on the twelfth of June, thirty-eight years ago, I have attended exactly seven obsequies in the edifice opposite. If I had my time again I should not put in an appearance at any one of them.

MARTIN

You've been in Chapel more than seven times, you know, Winslow.

WINSLOW

My dear boy?

MARTIN

Electing the Master and so on.

WINSLOW

I grant you I've been inside the building four times for that purpose. Three of which showed the College, in its collective wisdom, choosing the wrong candidate. Now I come to think of it, by this time next year I shall have to go inside the building again for the same purpose. My dear Tutor, have you worked out when the election falls due?

MARTIN

December the twentieth.

WINSLOW

Yes, well, I suppose I shall have to assist, in the French sense, at that ceremony. But I'm happy to say that this time I can't see even this College being so imbecile as to make a wrong choice. Francis Getliffe will do it very well.

SKEFFINGTON

I seem to remember having heard Arthur Brown's name mentioned.

WINSLOW

My dear Skeffington, Arthur Brown's name was mentioned last time. Largely, I fear, by Arthur Brown.

LEWIS

Getliffe is generally agreed on, is he?

WINSLOW

I've scarcely thought the matter worth conversation. The worthy Brown is patently a non-starter by the side of Francis Getliffe.

GAY

(*Who has suddenly woken up*)

You've forgotten me.

WINSLOW

My dear Gay, I had no idea you were planning to stand for the Mastership.

GAY

Mastership? No, no. The port. You've missed me out. Where is the port?

(*The port is passed, and he fills his glass.*)

Thank you, thank you. Ah! Port. There's a drink and a half, if ever there was one.

(*He drinks.*)

Capital.

(*To* LEWIS)

Excuse me. Do you mind telling me your name?

LEWIS
I'm Lewis Eliot.

GAY
Indeed. Have you any connection with the College?

LEWIS
I'm a former Fellow.

GAY
I congratulate you. Let me persuade you, sir, to have a glass of this excellent wine.

(*To the room at large*)

I don't know whether you realize it, but this is positively my last appearance before my annual hibernation. Yes, each year I hibernate for the worst of the winter. Indeed I do. You won't see me in College again till the spring. I am no longer as young as I used to be. So I retire to my own inglenook for the winter, and I listen to the great gales roaring over the Fens and I say to myself, "That's a gale and a half. I'd rather be where I am than out at sea."

TOM
It's damn nearly as bad in the summer these days.

GAY
What's that? What does he say?

MARTIN
It's been a bad summer this year.

GAY

Nonsense, my dear chap. You young men don't know what a bad summer is. Now '98, that was a bad summer. That was a summer and a half, I can tell you. I was in Iceland that summer. I was just getting into the swim of what some critics have been kind enough to call my great work on the Sagas. Great work—ah, indeed. Mind you, I've always disclaimed the word "great." I've always said, call the work distinguished if you like, but it's not for me to approve of the higher appellation. However, they insisted. —Where was I?

WINSLOW

In Iceland.

GAY

Precisely. That's where I was, that bitter summer of '98. And do you know what I found when I got there? Why, it was fifteen degrees warmer in Rejkjavik than in our unfortunate Cambridge!

(*To* LEWIS)

Do you mind telling me your name?

LEWIS

I'm Lewis Eliot.

GAY

Have you any connection with the College?

LEWIS

I'm a former Fellow.

GAY

I congratulate you. Well, I must be on my way.

(*He struggles up.*)

I wonder if two of you young men would be kind enough to escort me to a taxi.

(MARTIN *and* SKEFFINGTON *take an arm each.*)

Ah, thank you. Thank you indeed.

(*To* LEWIS)

Don't tell me!

(*Triumphantly*)

Eliot! Lewis Eliot! Ha! You see! I've got you taped! Well, good-night, my dear chap. And good-bye to you all—good-bye till the spring. Good-bye till the spring, Good-bye, good-bye. . . .

(*Assisted by* MARTIN *and* SKEFFINGTON, GAY *totters out.*)

WINSLOW

Let us hope that spring will be a little late this year.

(*He goes out after* GAY.)

TOM

(*As soon as they are alone*)

Lewis, I've been wanting to say this all evening. I really do most humbly apologise for—

(ARTHUR BROWN, *the Senior Tutor, hurries in through an inner door, which leads to the Master's Lodge.* BROWN *is sixty-three, plump and a bit of a buffer, but shrewd and obstinate. He carries his gown.*)

BROWN

(*Warmly, to* LEWIS)

My dear old friend!

LEWIS

Arthur!

BROWN

Getliffe told me you were here, but the Master had the Vice-Chancellor to dinner, and I was co-opted for coffee. Ah, but it's good to see you in this room again.

LEWIS

Thank you, Arthur.

BROWN

How's Margaret and the boy?

LEWIS

Both well. Both staying with Martin in the Queen's Road.

BROWN

Splendid. And the work—how are things in Whitehall?

LEWIS

Keeping me busy. Margaret says too busy.

BROWN

(*Affectionately*)

You never could say no to anyone, could you?

TOM

No, and, Lewis, that's what I wanted to say. You were most frightfully good about Laura Howard. It was monstrous of me to inflict her on you like that.

BROWN

(*Still genial, but suddenly alert*)

What's that? How did Lewis come to be meeting Mrs. Howard?

TOM

My fault, Arthur. She was wanting me to raise Cain in the College about her husband, so I shuffled her off onto Lewis. Mind you, Arthur, if I thought there was the slightest bit of sense in her case, I'd have come and told you straight out that I was going to bring it up. I do mean that. I think it's very important that people of my age should be ready to throw their weight about. I know you agree, Arthur, don't you?

BROWN

Yes, dear boy. Bless you—

(*Firmly*)

And goodnight to you, dear boy.

TOM

Eh?

BROWN

Goodnight.

TOM

Oh. Well, goodnight, Lewis.

LEWIS

Goodnight, Tom.

TOM

Goodnight, Arthur.

BROWN

Bless you, dear boy. Sleep you well.

(TOM *goes out.*)

(*Easily, pouring a glass of port*)

So our young friend has been involving you with the Howards, has he?

LEWIS

I'm not involved.

BROWN

Good. Good. Keep it that way, there's a good chap.

LEWIS

You've been having rather more trouble than I thought, haven't you?

**BROWN**

It's a wretched business. There's only one good thing to be said. The whole College was absolutely solid about it. I don't need to tell you that's not exactly common form.

**LEWIS**

What's this man Howard like, Arthur?

**BROWN**

(*With sudden passion*)

He's an unmitigated swine.

(*Controlling himself*)

No, I don't think I feel inclined to withdraw what I've just said. He's a twister, but there are plenty of twisters that have some redeeming qualities. I can't recall this chap showing a single one. He's graceless, he's never been able to get on with anyone, and I shouldn't be surprised if that's why he wants to pull the world down round our ears. I might have been able even to put up with that if he hadn't behaved so vilely to the people he owed everything to. He's a no good, Lewis. I don't mind telling you that I considered at the time, and I still do, we ought to have gone the whole hog and struck his name off the books.

(SIR FRANCIS GETLIFFE *comes in from the Lodge, followed by* NIGHTINGALE, *the Bursar of the College.* GETLIFFE *is a fine-featured man of fifty,* NIGHTINGALE *a well-preserved fifty-nine.*)

**GETLIFFE**

Whose name ought we to have struck off the books?

**BROWN**

Ah, there you are, Francis.

(*Pouring wine*)

A glass?

**GETLIFFE**

If I'm not intruding.

LEWIS

We were discussing the Howard affair, Francis. Tom Orbell introduced me to his wife the other day.

GETLIFFE

Did he now? She's a pretty girl, isn't she?

LEWIS

She was crying out loud that there'd been a miscarriage of justice. I suppose that's all nonsense?

NIGHTINGALE

(*Firmly*)

Quite nonsense. Good evening, Eliot.

LEWIS

Bursar.

GETLIFFE

There's nothing in that.

LEWIS

She seemed to think that he'd been turned out because of some sort of prejudice, which I never got quite clear.

GETLIFFE

That's simple. Howard was, and I suppose still is, a moderately well-known fellow-traveller.

BROWN

(*At once*)

I need hardly tell you that that had nothing to do with our decision.

GETLIFFE

No, if I'd thought that was deciding anything, I should have made a noise.

(*To* LEWIS)

I don't have to tell you that, do I?

NIGHTINGALE

One moment. Ought we to be discussing this while Eliot is with us?

LEWIS

I'm not quite a stranger, Nightingale.

NIGHTINGALE

I'm sorry. I believe no one outside the College should have heard a word.

LEWIS

I heard more than a word from Howard's wife. I can't for the life of me see how you're going to keep her quiet.

NIGHTINGALE

(*Deliberately*)

I trust we shall all of us keep quiet enough for our purposes.

(*He goes out.*)

LEWIS

Bad mark from the Bursar. Careless talk.

BROWN

Alec doesn't mean you, old chap. But he's right to be cautious. I don't want to exaggerate, but we could very easily have walked into trouble outside over this. It's just the sort of thing that could get into the Press, and if that happened, it could do the College more harm than I care to contemplate.

LEWIS

But keeping it a secret as you have done, if the story did leak, wouldn't you be in a worse mess than ever?

BROWN

We took the risk into account.

(MARTIN *and* SKEFFINGTON *return.*)

SKEFFINGTON
We finally got old Gay into a taxi.

MARTIN
Whether he'll ever get out is, of course, another matter.

(*They replenish their wine glasses.*)

BROWN

(*To* LEWIS)

I have some papers to finish. Drop in for a nightcap on your way to bed?

LEWIS
Not tonight, Arthur. I have to be up at six to play bears.

BROWN

(*Affectionately, with a hint of envy*)

Lucky, lucky Lewis. Sleep you well.

(*He goes out.* LEWIS *looks thoughtfully after him.*)

LEWIS
Brown's one of the kindest men I know, but Howard wouldn't be his favourite character, would he?

SKEFFINGTON
Howard?

MARTIN
Donald Howard wasn't anyone's favourite character. He was disliked inside the College, and with most of them his politics made them dislike him even more. But that wasn't the reason he was thrown out.

GETLIFFE
No. It was a reason, if you like, why we scientists found it difficult to get him elected in the first place. We had to be pretty rough with

them, and tell them that, politics or no politics, they mustn't shut
their eyes to an Alpha man.

MARTIN

In which we don't seem to have done superlatively well.

SKEFFINGTON

No, it was an ugly business. Only the worst sort of Red would have
done a thing like that.

LEWIS

Does that come in?

SKEFFINGTON

What I mean is, if the man had had anything to keep him straight—
if he'd had a faith—he might have done lots of bad things. He would
never have done the thing he did.

LEWIS

Exactly what did he do?

(*A moment—then:*)

GETLIFFE

He went in for a piece of simple, unadulterated fraud.

MARTIN

He faked the thesis which got him his Fellowship.

LEWIS

Faked? In what way?

MARTIN

One of the diffraction photographs in his paper—the decisive photograph in his experimental evidence—was a forgery.

LEWIS

There's no doubt?

MARTIN
None.


LEWIS
What put you on to it?


GETLIFFE
Some Americans working in the same field. When Howard's paper was published it was attacked by them on the grounds that the experimental results couldn't be repeated.


SKEFFINGTON
Nightingale and I were asked by the College to look into it and report. There was no question. His key diffraction photograph was a fraud.


LEWIS
Could the fraud have been accidental?


GETLIFFE
No. It was only too straightforward. The photograph had been blown up—enlarged to look like the result of a totally different experiment.


LEWIS
How was it detected?


SKEFFINGTON
When they examined the enlargement made from the original negative, the hole left by a drawing-pin, which had held the negative up to dry, was blown up, too.


GETLIFFE
The Americans asked why the white blob at the top of the photograph was so singularly large.

MARTIN

It was a clear case. The Court of Seniors had no option but to kick him out.

LEWIS

Who sat on the Court?

MARTIN

The Master, of course. Brown, old Winslow, and Nightingale, in his capacity as Bursar.

GETLIFFE

Of course they had to go on what we scientists told them. Nightingale's the only one of them who'd have any idea what a diffraction photograph was. But they went into it all very thoroughly.

LEWIS

How thoroughly?

MARTIN

They interviewed Howard.

GETLIFFE

Twice.

LEWIS

What was his explanation?

MARTIN

He simply denied that there *was* any fraud.

GETLIFFE

So the Master and Brown wrote formally, telling him to put his case on paper.

MARTIN

He still produced no explanation. Then he suddenly asked to appear before the Court again and announced that he had now decided that there *had* been a fraud, but the fraud wasn't his, it was old Palairet's.

SKEFFINGTON

Which must have taken some cooking-up.

LEWIS

Old Palairet?

MARTIN

His professor.

GETLIFFE

Howard's paper was published in collaboration with Palairet. They worked on it together.

LEWIS

Palairet. Palairet. I know the name.

GETLIFFE

You should. He was one of the top men of his day.

LEWIS

Wasn't he once a Fellow here?

GETLIFFE

In his early days, yes. Then he went off to Aberdeen and had a long and brilliant career there. Skeffington knew him.

SKEFFINGTON

We're related by marriage. My wife is his niece.

LEWIS

And Howard accused Palairet of fraud?

SKEFFINGTON

He did.

LEWIS

What did Palairet say?

SKEFFINGTON

Nothing. He couldn't. You see, he'd just died.

MARTIN

Leaving a nice little bequest to the College. His entire estate. Thirty-five thousand.

SKEFFINGTON

Yes, it was a smack in the eye for the family.

LEWIS

I see. Accusing Palairet after that could hardly have endeared Howard to the Seniors.

GETLIFFE

It didn't.

MARTIN

All the same, although his story was the most improbable anyone could have invented, they insisted they must act as though it might be true.

SKEFFINGTON

If it were, there would almost certainly be signs of faked evidence in the old boy's notebooks. Howard himself claimed that Palairet had shown him identical photographs to his published print. So Palairet's executors were asked to turn over to the College all his scientific papers.

GETLIFFE

As he'd left us his estate, that was quite in order.

SKEFFINGTON

They arrived in batches. It was about as likely we should find anything wrong as that one of us would be nabbed in the buttery pinching a case of Scotch, but Nightingale and I went through the lot.

GETLIFFE
So did Martin, and so did I.


MARTIN
We studied every one of the old man's diffraction photographs, millimetre by millimetre.


LEWIS
And found nothing?


MARTIN
And found nothing.


SKEFFINGTON
So that was that. Fair enough?


LEWIS
No court of law could have been fairer.


GETLIFFE
You know, considering the chances and the temptation, there've
been astonishingly few scientific frauds. There was Rupp, of course,
the G-phenomenon—but that was probably an honest mistake.


SKEFFINGTON
What staggers me is how a man of science could do such a thing. I
mean, it's a denial of everything he lives for—or ought to live for.


GETLIFFE
There's no mystery why Howard did it. He just wanted to make his
marble good.


LEWIS
You're all absolutely sure, beyond any possible shadow of doubt,
that he did it? Skeffington?

SKEFFINGTON

As sure as I am that there's a God in heaven.

LEWIS

Martin?

MARTIN

Yes.

LEWIS

Francis?

GETLIFFE

Oh yes. Oh yes, he did it all right!

*THE CURTAIN FALLS.*

# ACT ONE

## Scene 3

LEWIS ELIOT'S FLAT IN LONDON

*A Sunday afternoon.* MARGARET ELIOT, LEWIS'S *wife, a quiet, pretty, intelligent woman, sits at a writing desk, writing a letter. On the desk is a house telephone. After a moment, it buzzes.*

MARGARET

(*She picks up the receiver.*)

Hello. Yes, it is. Who is that? Oh. Good afternoon.

LEWIS

(*Entering*)

If that's for me, I'm out.

MARGARET

No, I'm sorry, he's out. Yes, quite sure. Oh. Oh, I see. Well then, yes, he is, but he's very tired. Yes, I can get him if it's really necessary, but are you certain it can't wait?

LEWIS

(*In an undertone*)

Who is it?

49

MARGARET

(*Into house phone*)

Will you hold on?

(*She covers the mouthpiece.*)

It's Mrs. Howard. She's downstairs.

LEWIS

I'm away.

MARGARET

She saw you come in. They've been waiting in the doorway opposite.

LEWIS

They?

MARGARET

She's got her husband with her. She wants to know if they can come up.

LEWIS

No.

MARGARET

What shall I say?

LEWIS

I'm sick. It's highly infectious. Measles or something.

MARGARET

Lewis, they've come up to London specially, darling, I think you'll have to see them.

LEWIS

I'm under no obligation to spend five minutes with either of them.

MARGARET

I know, but they're here. —Yes?


LEWIS

(*Exasperated*)

Oh . . . I suppose so.


MARGARET

(*Into phone*)

All right. We're on the first floor. Oh.

(*Hangs up*)

She says she knows.


LEWIS

This is intolerable. What the hell does she mean, hanging around doorways, spying on me?


MARGARET

See them just this once and get it over. Then you've done everything anyone can possibly expect.


LEWIS

I wrote and told her I can't help. What more am I supposed to do?


MARGARET

Meet her man and change your mind.


LEWIS

It won't.


MARGARET

Five minutes. Then out.

LEWIS

This affair is nothing to do with me. Why am I pestered?

MARGARET

You have a kind face.

LEWIS

I do not have a kind face.

MARGARET

I think so.

LEWIS

In future I shall wear a permanent scowl.

MARGARET

You wouldn't know how, my darling.

(*She kisses him lightly. The doorbell rings.*)

There they are. Be pleasant, now.

(*She goes into the hall.*)

(*Off*)

Hello. Will you come in?

LAURA

(*Off*)

Thanks.

MARGARET

(*Off*)

My husband's in here.

(*She returns, with* LAURA *and* DONALD HOWARD. HOWARD *is un-prepossessing—a long nose, not much chin, a coarse, pale skin. He seems especially unattractive by the side of his wife. His manner is sullen, farouche.*)

LEWIS
Well. This is a surprise.

LAURA
A deliberate one. If you'd had warning, would you have seen us? This is Donald.

LEWIS
Good afternoon.

(HOWARD *just nods.*)

MARGARET
Won't you sit down?

(*They sit.*)

LAURA
I'm sorry if we've come at an awkward time. Sunday is Donald's only free day.

LEWIS
It's mine too.

LAURA
You're more or less your own boss, aren't you? Donald has to clock in.

LEWIS
Where?

HOWARD
Romsey Grammar School.

LAURA
He's got a job there. Physics master.

LEWIS
I'm glad.

HOWARD
It's temporary.

LAURA
Their man's away ill.

(*Pause*)

MARGARET
Can I get you some tea?

LAURA
We had it at the station. When we got here the porter said you were out.

LEWIS
I was.

LAURA
So we waited.

LEWIS
Yes.

(*Pause. To* LAURA)

A drink?

LAURA
No, thanks.

LEWIS
Howard?

HOWARD
I believe you know that chap Luke.

LEWIS
Walter Luke? Yes, he's an old friend of mine.

HOWARD
Is he? You must be an extraordinary man. . . .

LEWIS
Oh? Why?

HOWARD
He's got a finger in this bomb nonsense, hasn't he? I don't know how
a scientist can bring himself to do it.

LEWIS
He happens to think it's his duty.

HOWARD
Huh!

(*Pause*)

LAURA

(*To* LEWIS)

I got your letter.

LEWIS
Yes?

LAURA
You didn't say much.

LEWIS
I'm afraid there wasn't much to say.

LAURA
You talked to them?

LEWIS
At some length.

LAURA

(*To* MARGARET)

How much have you heard about this difficulty of ours?

MARGARET

Roughly what Lewis has.

LAURA

Then you can understand why we're utterly sickened by the whole crowd of them!

MARGARET

(*Carefully*)

I think I can understand how you feel.

HOWARD

Can you?

MARGARET

Yes. I'll leave you with Lewis.

(*She goes out quickly, closing the door.*)

LAURA

So they're still shilly-shallying, are they?

LEWIS

What about?

LAURA

Re-opening the case.

LEWIS

No.

LAURA

What do you mean?

LEWIS

I mean that, so far as I heard, no one has the slightest intention of re-opening the case.

LAURA

(*Angrily, to* HOWARD)

Do you believe that?

HOWARD

I shouldn't be surprised.

LAURA

(*To* LEWIS)

Would you be content with that, if you were there?

LEWIS

I'm afraid I haven't heard anything that would make me take any steps.

LAURA

What right have you got to say that!

LEWIS

I can't take any other view, in the light of what the scientists report about the evidence.

LAURA

And you accept what the scientists say?

LEWIS

I must. I'm quite unqualified to analyse it myself, and so are most of the people in the College. If I were there, I should have to believe what Francis Getliffe and the others told me.

LAURA

Oh, we know all about Getliffe. . . .

LEWIS

No, I can't listen to that. Francis Getliffe has been a friend of mine for twenty-five years.

LAURA

Well?

LEWIS

I trust him completely. So would anyone who knew him.

HOWARD

(*In a sneering tone*)

Getliffe is a good example of a man who used to be a progressive and has thought better of it.

LEWIS

I shouldn't have thought that was true. If it were, it would make no difference to his judgment.

HOWARD

I'd like to know what would.

LEWIS

You must know what would. And that is what he thought, as a scientist, of the evidence under his eyes.

HOWARD

I suppose they weren't prejudiced when I gave them the explanation!

LEWIS

I've heard exactly what they did about that.

HOWARD

Who from?

LEWIS
Getliffe—Skeffington—

LAURA
Skeffington! Do you think *he* wasn't prejudiced?

LEWIS
I don't know Skeffington as I know Getliffe, but he strikes me as an honest man.

HOWARD
He's a Catholic, a religious maniac, the worst snob in the College.

LEWIS
I also talked to my brother.

LAURA
Martin! Do you think Martin would lift a finger against the hierarchy? All he wants is to step into old Brown's shoes, if Brown gets the Mastership next year.

LEWIS
Even if that were true, my brother had nothing to do with the Court's decision.

LAURA
He also did nothing to change it.

HOWARD
He let them believe what they wanted to believe.

LEWIS
Are you saying now that you weren't given a fair hearing?

HOWARD
What do you think?

(*Pause*)

LEWIS

(*Controlling himself with an effort*)

Since you're here, I'd like to clear up one or two points, simply for my own satisfaction. May I?

(HOWARD *moves away but* LAURA *restrains him. He turns to* LEWIS.)

HOWARD

Go on.

LEWIS

According to my information, you appeared before the Court of Seniors three times. Is that right?

HOWARD

I suppose it was three.

LEWIS

The first time you were told that the scientists had decided that one of the photographs in your paper was a fraud. Were you told that?

HOWARD

I suppose that's what it amounted to.

LEWIS

It must have been clear one way or the other, mustn't it? Were you told in so many words the photograph was a fraud?

HOWARD

Yes, I suppose I was.

LEWIS

Was it a fraud?

HOWARD

I don't know what you mean.

LEWIS
What I say. Was that photograph a fraud? That is, was it faked to prove something in your paper?

HOWARD
I suppose you could say that.

LEWIS
Is there any shadow of doubt whatsoever?

(*Pause*)

HOWARD
No.

LEWIS
Did you agree with the Court of Seniors when they told you it was a fraud?

HOWARD
Yes.

LEWIS
My information is that you denied it totally the first couple of times that you appeared before them.

HOWARD
I told them eventually.

LEWIS
On your third appearance.

HOWARD
Yes.

LEWIS
Why did you deny it before?

HOWARD

Because I didn't believe it was true.

LEWIS

Yet every other scientist who saw the evidence didn't take long to be certain it was true.

HOWARD

They were glad of the chance to find something against me.

LEWIS

Why did you take so long to be certain? Here was this photograph. You must have known it very well. But even when you'd been told about it, you still didn't admit that it was a fraud. Why not?

(*No answer*)

All right. Finally you decided it was a fraud.

HOWARD

I've said so.

LEWIS

And then you produced an explanation.

HOWARD

Yes.

LEWIS

What was it?

HOWARD

You must have picked up that with all the other information they've given you.

LEWIS

In fact, you blamed the fraud on your collaborator? A man who'd just died, at the age of, what was it, seventy-five?

**HOWARD**

What's his age got to do with anything?

**LEWIS**

Your explanation was that *he* had faked the photograph in *your* paper?

**HOWARD**

Yes.

**LEWIS**

Did that seem to you likely?

**LAURA**

Of course it didn't.

(*To* HOWARD)

You had a great respect for him—of course you had.

**LEWIS**

Did you have a great respect for him?

**HOWARD**

Not specially.

**LEWIS**

What reason did you think he could have, at that age, and in his position, for such a fraud?

**HOWARD**

Your guess is as good as mine.

**LEWIS**

What did you think of him as a person?

**HOWARD**

I didn't have anything to do with him apart from the work. He was always decent to me.

LEWIS

What did other people think of him?

HOWARD

I don't give a damn what other people think about other people. I take them as I find them and by how they are to me.

LEWIS

(*Dryly*)

And you're satisfied with the result?

HOWARD

Look, I'm not a lawyer. It's no use asking me to cook up a pretty story.

LEWIS

(*Sharply*)

That isn't especially valuable, even in Law. . . . You told the Court that Palairet gave you the print with the pin-marks—the one you used in your thesis.

HOWARD

So he did.

LEWIS

Why should he do that?

HOWARD

He said it would help out the experimental evidence.

LEWIS

And you never wondered for an instant whether it was genuine?

HOWARD

I took it for granted.

**LEWIS**

Why?

**HOWARD**

He was a big noise. It never occurred to me there might be something wrong.

**LEWIS**

It never occurred to you.

**HOWARD**

That's what I said.

**LEWIS**

And you're a scientist?

**HOWARD**

I was.

(*Pause*)

**LEWIS**

Howard, when you finally admitted that the photograph in your paper was a fraud, you also claimed that Palairet had shown you identical prints of the same photograph before. Did you say that?

**HOWARD**

Yes.

**LEWIS**

Who had made those prints?

**HOWARD**

The old man, of course.

**LEWIS**

How many had you seen?

HOWARD
I can't remember.

LEWIS
Many?

HOWARD
No.

LEWIS
Only one?

HOWARD
I don't know.

LEWIS
You're sure you saw one? At least one more, besides yours?

HOWARD
I've told you I did.

LEWIS
Did you know there were no signs of any such photographs in the whole of Palairet's scientific notebooks?

HOWARD
I suppose they told me that.

LEWIS
They must have told you.

HOWARD
All right, they told me. What I want to know is, who looked?

(*Pause*)

LEWIS
Thank you. That's all.

(*He turns away to his desk as if dismissing the conversation.*)

LAURA
You mean you're satisfied now?

LEWIS
I mean I don't think it's any use going further.

LAURA
Then you'll go back and talk to them again? Getliffe and the others?

LEWIS
What do you think I could possibly say?

LAURA
Tell them they've got to re-open the case.

LEWIS
They wouldn't listen.

LAURA
How do you know unless you try?

LEWIS
There's nothing I could say to make them. They've gone into it all with the utmost care.

LAURA
Care!

LEWIS
No body of men could have been more punctilious.

LAURA
No body of men could have been more bigoted.

HOWARD
They'd made up their minds to do me down. This gave them an opportunity and they jumped at it.

LEWIS

That's just not true.

LAURA

There must be a way to force their hand. What makes a Court of Law re-open a case?

LEWIS

Fresh evidence, if it's strong enough.

LAURA

If it were strong enough, and the College came across it, they'd suppress it in the name of *pax academica*. I know them.

LEWIS

I really think you'd better go now.

(HOWARD *turns abruptly away.* LAURA *restrains him, then crosses to* LEWIS. HOWARD *remains impassive in the doorway.*)

LAURA

Look, his Fellowship has nine months to run. He's lost another nine already. Do you know what a year and a half, at a time like this, means to a man like Donald? It's not the money, though God knows we could do with it. It's everything a Fellowship stands for. It's reputation, it's opportunity, it's all the facilities for research that a university has to offer a scientist. It's the whole foundation of his career. That's what they've taken away from him.

LEWIS

I'm sorry.

LAURA

It's not enough to be sorry! There must be something you can do to help.

HOWARD

(*Roughly*)

Why the hell should he help? Can't you see? He doesn't believe me any more than the others.

LAURA

Of course he does. He must!

(*To* LEWIS)

You do believe him, don't you? Tell him you believe him!

(*Pause*)

HOWARD

Come on.

(*He goes out without a word.* LAURA *follows. The front door slams. In a moment,* MARGARET *re-enters.*)

LEWIS

Well . . . no one could call that a particularly agreeable party.

MARGARET

(*Shutting the door and crossing to* LEWIS)

Were you rough with him, darling?

LEWIS

I had to be.

MARGARET

(*With a smile*)

That's not quite all, is it?

LEWIS

(*Smiles back*)

He's not exactly my cup of tea.

MARGARET

Whereas, if he hadn't done what he unfortunately has done, you wouldn't be surprised if I thought he had a sort of integrity, would you?

LEWIS

Yes, I would.

MARGARET

Whatever else he is, I don't think he's two-faced.

LEWIS

What good's that, when the one face he has got is so peculiarly unpleasant?

MARGARET

I'm still not clear why what he did was wrong. I mean, why can't a scientist enlarge a photograph the same as the next man?

LEWIS

No reason at all—provided he acknowledges the enlargement. Let me put it to you in the simplest terms—

MARGARET

(*With a smile*)

Thank you, darling.

LEWIS

(*Seating himself on the arm of her chair*)

If you enlarge a sardine to look like a salmon, you don't call it a salmon, you call it a sardine—enlarged—unless you want the world to call you a liar.

MARGARET

And that's what Howard's supposed to have done?

LEWIS

No. That's what he did.

MARGARET

He says he didn't.

LEWIS

He's lying.

MARGARET
What makes you so sure?

LEWIS
I'm a lawyer, Meg. I know a lie when I hear one.

(*The telephone rings.* LEWIS *rises and answers it.*)

Yes? Oh, Martin. All right, a bit tired.

(*He stiffens suddenly. There is a long pause.*)

Skeffington?

(*Another long pause. Finally—*)

All right.

(*He hangs up abruptly and stands quite still.*)

I've got to go to Cambridge.

MARGARET
It's Howard, isn't it?

LEWIS
Yes. Skeffington says he's been telling the truth.

(*As he starts for the door—*)

*CURTAIN*

ACT TWO

# ACT TWO

*Scene 1*

MARTIN ELIOT'S ROOMS IN COLLEGE. THE NEXT DAY

*A microscope, slides, various scientific impedimenta are on the desk where he is seated, speaking on the College internal telephone, as the curtain rises.*

MARTIN

Yes, it is urgent. Shall we say a quarter of an hour? My rooms—yes. Thanks, Alec.

(*He puts the receiver down as* LEWIS *enters the room, dressed in an overcoat and carrying a hat.*)

(*To* LEWIS)

Ah! Lewis. Good. Sorry to drag you back like this. I suppose I've ruined your weekend?

LEWIS

You have, dear brother, you have. Where's Skeffington?

MARTIN

I'll call him.

(*He picks up the receiver of the internal telephone and presses the buzzer and, while waiting for a reply, turns to* LEWIS.)

I've been on to Francis and Alec too, but I want you to see Julian first—

(*Into telephone*)

Julian, Lewis is here. My rooms, yes. Can you come straight over? Good.

(*He replaces the receiver.*)

He's coming.

75

LEWIS

Is he right?

MARTIN

It makes more sense than any other explanation.

LEWIS

I wish I could follow the evidence better. I suppose understanding makes it easier?

MARTIN

It's still very hard to take.

LEWIS

Yes.

(*Pause*)

Martin, before the others come, there's something I want to say.

MARTIN

I think I know what it is—but say it.

LEWIS

If Skeffington talks, there'll be a row.

MARTIN

That's putting it mildly.

LEWIS

(*Bluntly*)

Do you have to get into it?

MARTIN

I don't *have* to, no. In fact, if I don't want to quarrel with half the College, I'd better not. Isn't that what you wanted to say?

LEWIS

I think you should be . . . rather careful.

MARTIN

(*Wryly*)

That's my nature. *You* know that.

LEWIS

It's not your business, is it?

MARTIN

No.

LEWIS

Whose is it?

MARTIN

Constitutionally, it would be for the Sub-Committee who made the original report to take the first steps.

LEWIS

That's Nightingale and Skeffington himself.

MARTIN

Yes.

LEWIS

Then if he's right, Skeffington can't avoid some sort of commitment.

MARTIN

I think he'd have to do something for Howard.

LEWIS

He's a Catholic, isn't he?

MARTIN

Skeffington? Yes. But that won't stop him. Justice for the enemy.

(SKEFFINGTON *strides in. He has with him a thick exercise book.*)

SKEFFINGTON

(*Briskly, to* LEWIS)

I'm glad you're here. Now what's the first move?

LEWIS

To be sure you're right. How sure are you?

SKEFFINGTON

I tell you, he's been telling the truth.

LEWIS

Can you prove it?

SKEFFINGTON

Enough to satisfy myself.

LEWIS

That's not what I asked. Have you got one-hundred per cent proof that will satisfy everybody else?

(*Pause*)

SKEFFINGTON

I'm not sure that I have. But it should be enough for reasonable people.

LEWIS

What do you intend to do?

SKEFFINGTON

The first thing is to get the man a square deal. That goes without question.

LEWIS

When did you decide that?

SKEFFINGTON

The moment I realized there was only one answer to this business.

**LEWIS**

And that was—when?

**SKEFFINGTON**

Yesterday afternoon.

**MARTIN**

I'm sorry, Julian, but it's not so easy to accept that there can't be some other explanation.

**SKEFFINGTON**

Don't you think I've made sure that I've closed all the holes?

**LEWIS**

Don't you think you might be wrong? After all, you're saying you've been wrong once before, aren't you?

**SKEFFINGTON**

You'll see that I'm not wrong.

**MARTIN**

Tell Lewis what you've told me.

**LEWIS**

And go carefully—remember, I'm not a scientist.

**SKEFFINGTON**

(*To* LEWIS)

Ever since old Palairet's death, his scientific papers have been arriving at the College. His executor sent them at irregular intervals. There were weeks, sometimes months, between batches. On Saturday, I heard from the Bursar that a final box had arrived. I was mildly surprised. I imagined—we all did—that we already had the lot. I didn't think a great deal to it, but in the circumstances I thought I'd better make a routine check. So I went to the Bursary, opened the box, and took the papers back to my rooms. It was old man's stuff, mostly. Notes on researches he never did, sets of data, corrections and so on. Halfway through I came on this.

*(He picks up the exercise book. Sticking out of it is a book-marker. He opens it at the place marked.)*

At first I didn't take in what it meant. I was sitting in my rooms in the Fellows' Building, and I went out and walked in the garden, and I couldn't see anything that made sense. Then it hit me. Listen.

*(He reads from the book.)*

"July 20th, 1957. Tried diffraction experiments using neutron source A, and crystal grating B. Encouraging results."

LEWIS
If that's important, I'm lost already.

SKEFFINGTON
Wait. After that there's a blank space with a rim of sticky paper round it, where there's obviously been some sort of photograph. There.

*(He turns the book round and holds it up for* LEWIS *to see.)*

Underneath where the photograph was, there's this:

*(He reads again from the book.)*

"Above print gives strong support for view that diffraction of neutrons at higher speeds, corresponding to wave-lengths shown above, follows precisely the same pattern as at low speeds. Have always predicted this. Follow up."

LEWIS
That's Palairet's handwriting?

SKEFFINGTON
Of course.

LEWIS
And the photograph's missing?

MARTIN
If there ever was one there.

SKEFFINGTON

(*Forcefully*)

The point is that what the caption says is untrue. The old man was fooling himself. It was Howard's extension of this very thing that the Americans proved was impossible. It's just not true. *And that's where Howard's paper starts off.*

LEWIS

You mean he was quoting his master's voice?

SKEFFINGTON

It speaks for itself.

LEWIS

Then his story stands up?

SKEFFINGTON

I can't see any other conclusion.

(*Pause*)

LEWIS

(*To* MARTIN)

Can you?

MARTIN

(*Carefully*)

If the print were there—I don't think I could. You see, either it couldn't have shown anything at all—or else *that* print had been blown up too.

LEWIS

You agree that what the caption says is untrue?

MARTIN

Oh yes. We know now it couldn't be true.

LEWIS
At the time, could Howard have believed it to be true?

MARTIN
Assuming he trusted his professor blindly—and assuming the print supported the caption.

(*Pause*)

SKEFFINGTON
What I can't understand is *why* the old boy did it. It couldn't have done him two-pennorth of good. His position was beyond dispute. Compared with his established work, this experiment was totally un-important.

MARTIN
I can't believe there isn't an alternative answer.

SKEFFINGTON
Do you think I *want* to believe there isn't? It's not exactly pleasant for me to stir up mud about someone connected with my family, and, if I had to, I shouldn't choose to do it on behalf of anyone like How-ard, who stands for just about everything I abominate. We ought never to have let in a Red like that. But the point is we did, and I believe him innocent.

MARTIN
Yes, Julian. We know *you* believe that. It's like G. H. Hardy's old crack: "If the Archbishop of Canterbury says he believes in God, that's all in the way of business, but if he says he doesn't, you can take it he means what he says." But I don't see that recognizing your conviction gets us very far.

SKEFFINGTON
It might, when I've settled what to do next.

MARTIN
I hope you don't do anything until we've thought it over.

SKEFFINGTON
I'm not waiting, if that's what you mean.

LEWIS

If you start something, there'll be a row.

SKEFFINGTON

I can't help that.

MARTIN

Now, listen, Julian—

SKEFFINGTON

Are you suggesting I should keep quiet about this?

MARTIN

I'm asking you to wait.

SKEFFINGTON

(*Tight-lipped*)

I'm sorry.

LEWIS

In that case, it seems to me there are just two courses you can take. You can write a statement to the Master saying, for the sake of argument, that some new technical data makes it extremely unlikely that Howard was responsible for any fraud. If I were you, I should have to do that.

SKEFFINGTON

I should think you damned well would.

MARTIN

I doubt if it would have any effect. The evidence isn't quite clinching enough to convince anyone who desperately doesn't want to be convinced. And there are quite a number of our friends who desperately don't want to be convinced.

SKEFFINGTON

They've got to be.

LEWIS

That's your second course. You set yourself, first, to get the case re-opened, and then, which isn't the same thing, to make the Seniors reverse their decision. I don't say it's impossible.

SKEFFINGTON

Thanks.

LEWIS

But it's going to be very, very difficult.

MARTIN

It's also going to need one or two qualities I'm not sure Julian possesses.

SKEFFINGTON

What does it need?

MARTIN

Obstinacy.

LEWIS

I'm prepared to credit him with that.

MARTIN

Patience.

LEWIS

(*To* SKEFFINGTON)

How do you fancy yourself in that respect?

MARTIN

Persuasive power.

SKEFFINGTON

That's where Lewis comes in.

LEWIS

I haven't said that I'm coming in.

MARTIN

And a considerable command of political tactics. It's going to take a good deal of internal politics to put Howard in the clear.

SKEFFINGTON

That's where *you* come in.

MARTIN

I haven't said I'm coming in, either.

SKEFFINGTON

(*Fiercely*)

All right, all right. I'll go it alone.

MARTIN

Julian, listen to me. This business can split the College from top to bottom. It can make the place unlivable in. You've got to live here.

SKEFFINGTON

I've also got to live with myself.

(*Pause*)

LEWIS

(*Casually*)

Is your Fellowship a permanent one?

SKEFFINGTON

(*Surprised*)

No.

LEWIS

But you'd like to be a fixture?

SKEFFINGTON

Yes.

LEWIS

Make trouble and you could damage your prospects. Oh, I don't mean they'd do anything flagrantly unjust. If you were a Rutherford or a Blackett, you could insult the Master every night of your life and they'd keep you on and bury you in Chapel.

MARTIN

But you're not that big, and neither am I. So if there's a cloud round the name of Skeffington they might say quietly, "Let him go." Just as they might think half a dozen people would do the Senior Tutorship as well or better than Martin Eliot.

SKEFFINGTON

What does all this add up to?

MARTIN

Merely that if they have anything against us, the net result is liable to be that Skeffington's out and M. F. Eliot doesn't get a promotion.

SKEFFINGTON

Do you seriously think that's going to stop me?

MARTIN

I just wanted you to know. If I'm going to take a risk myself, I like to calculate the chances beforehand.

LEWIS

And are you?

MARTIN

What?

LEWIS

Going to take a risk yourself?

(*Pause*)

MARTIN

(*Lightly*)

There's nothing for it. I shall have to help him.

SKEFFINGTON

(*Eagerly, seizing his hand*)

I knew it! Lewis?

(*Pause*)

LEWIS

There are always good, sound, human. sensitive reasons for contract-ing out. There's great dignity in being a spectator. And if you do it for long enough, you're dead inside. . . . I'll do what I can.

SKEFFINGTON

Right! Who do we tackle first?

LEWIS

Francis Getliffe. Get him active and all the others will have to listen.

MARTIN

Francis may not be easy.

SKEFFINGTON

He can't blink the evidence.

MARTIN

I wonder. The Mastership comes up in the autumn. You're asking him to divide the College at a time when he needs their united sup-port.

SKEFFINGTON

You don't think for one moment a thing like that would influence a man like Getliffe?

LEWIS

The Mastership matters to Francis. It's asking a lot.

(*Pause*)

SKEFFINGTON

Blast Howard to hell. If he'd had the scientific judgment of a newt he'd never have taken the old man's experiments on trust. It's almost unbelievable that anyone working in his field accepted them without double-checking.

LEWIS

"Unbelievable." But you believe it.

SKEFFINGTON

Yes, I believe it.

(*A tap on the door.* FRANCIS GETLIFFE *enters.*)

GETLIFFE

May I come in?

(*Warmly*)

Lewis! I didn't know you were here.

LEWIS

Francis. Martin asked me to come.

GETLIFFE

And me, and me. I imagined a scientific conclave, but as you're with us it must be social. So much the better. We talk far too much shop.

(*He takes out a pipe.*)

MARTIN

I'm afraid it's not social.

GETLIFFE

(*Easy, relaxed*)

No? What a pity! Well, then—what?

SKEFFINGTON

It's about the Howard affair. We've been blaming the wrong man.

GETLIFFE

(*Sharply*)

What's that?

SKEFFINGTON

I'd like you to see this notebook. It's Palairet's.

(*He opens the exercise book at the page marked by the book-marker and hands it to* GETLIFFE. *They watch in silence as* GET-LIFFE *studies it. At length he looks up.*)

GETLIFFE

(*In a harsh voice*)

Is that all?

SKEFFINGTON

I think it puts you in the picture.

GETLIFFE

It's just about the most incredible picture I ever heard of.

MARTIN

(*Deliberately conversational*)

You mean it's incredible that we've all been such fools?

GETLIFFE

(*Snapping*)

I should like to know when we stop being fools!

LEWIS

Listen, Francis—

GETLIFFE

One moment. Let me be clear about this. You're saying, on the strength of this entry, that Howard is innocent and Palairet is guilty of fraud?

LEWIS

In the face of the evidence, what else can one say?

GETLIFFE

(*Sharply*)

Lewis, you're not a scientist.

LEWIS

Then as a scientist you reject the implications?

GETLIFFE

If you're going to attack the memory of a distinguished old man, you'll want something firmer than implications.

SKEFFINGTON

The facts are firm.

MARTIN

At any rate, they're as firm as one could expect. If only that photograph weren't missing.

GETLIFFE

Presuming there was ever a photograph there.

MARTIN

Presuming that. Given that photograph, I should have thought there was enough evidence to satisfy a Court of Law. What do you think, Lewis?

LEWIS

It would be a terribly difficult case for an ordinary Court. So much would depend on the technical witnesses. But I agree with Martin. I believe that if that photograph weren't missing, a Court would probably see that Howard was cleared.

GETLIFFE

And without it?

LEWIS

Without it, in a Court of Law, I'd give him an even chance. . . .

(*Pause*)

GETLIFFE

(*Easily, more relaxed*)

This . . . explanation of yours is very hard to credit, you know.

SKEFFINGTON

Can you think of a better one?

GETLIFFE

I shouldn't have thought it was beyond the wit of man.

SKEFFINGTON

If we thought that, we shouldn't have involved you.

GETLIFFE

I'm not involved.

SKEFFINGTON

We're asking you to be.

MARTIN

Francis, we need a majority to re-open the case. With your support, we think we might just get it.

(*Pause*)

GETLIFFE

I see.

(*Pause. To* SKEFFINGTON)

Remind me who acted as referees on Howard's work when we elected him.

SKEFFINGTON

There was one external—Morrison. One internal—Nightingale. I was asked to write a note along with Nightingale's.

GETLIFFE

And you and Nightingale reported on his work when we dismissed him.

SKEFFINGTON

Yes.

GETLIFFE

What does Nightingale say about this? Or haven't you told him?

SKEFFINGTON

Yes, I saw him at once. He—

(*A knock at the door.* NIGHTINGALE *enters.*)

NIGHTINGALE

(*To* MARTIN)

I'm sorry I'm late. I had to polish off some conveyances.

(*To* LEWIS)

Ah, Eliot, back again?

LEWIS

I'm afraid so.

GETLIFFE

Alec, have you seen this?

(*He shows him the exercise book.*)

NIGHTINGALE

Yes, indeed. Skeffington brought it to my attention last night.

GETLIFFE

What did you make of it?

NIGHTINGALE

A storm in a crucible.

SKEFFINGTON

My God!

NIGHTINGALE

(*Calmly*)

I saw nothing which would make any difference to my original opinion. If I were writing my report to the Seniors again today, I should do so in the same terms.

SKEFFINGTON

(*Furiously*)

Then you'd be deliberately shutting your eyes to the truth.

NIGHTINGALE

That is not a habit of mine, Skeffington.

LEWIS

You're saying that, if this notebook had been available to the Court, the Court would have come to the same conclusion?

NIGHTINGALE

I am. The additional evidence, such as it is, is trivial and inconclusive.

SKEFFINGTON

I don't agree.

NIGHTINGALE

Then we must agree to differ, that's all.

SKEFFINGTON

No. That's not all. Not by a long chalk.

NIGHTINGALE

Am I to understand that you contemplate taking the matter further?

SKEFFINGTON

You don't think I'm leaving it here, do you?

NIGHTINGALE

(*Carefully*)

I think you would be very unwise to disturb the situation, Skeffington. In my view, anyone who resurrects this affair is taking a grave responsibility upon himself.

SKEFFINGTON

Anyone who buries it has a pretty peculiar sense of justice.

NIGHTINGALE

We on the Court did justice so far as we could. We have every reason to believe that our findings were the right ones.

SKEFFINGTON

The wrong ones.

NIGHTINGALE

The matter was thoroughly investigated and an unanimous decision reached by the Court. So far as I'm concerned, the subject is closed.

SKEFFINGTON

No.

MARTIN

It ought to be thrashed out, Alec.

NIGHTINGALE

Re-opening the affair will achieve nothing except harm for the College—and that, I know we should all agree, is the very last thing any of us wants. Had I known the possibility was to be considered, I should not have attended this meeting. You must excuse me.

(*He goes out.*)

SKEFFINGTON

Of all the canting hypocrisy!

MARTIN

Steady, Julian.

SKEFFINGTON

He hasn't got a leg to stand on! No one will listen to him!

LEWIS

I'm not so sure.

GETLIFFE

Neither am I. Nightingale knows as much as any, and more than most, about this business. If, after carefully weighing the pros and cons, he comes to the opposite conclusion to Skeffington, I'm fairly sure he won't be the only one.

LEWIS

Does that mean that you agree with him?

(*Pause*)

GETLIFFE

(*At length, with deliberation*)

I don't know that I'm required either to agree or to disagree. I did not sit on the Court. I made no report to it. I had little or nothing to do with its decision. Frankly, I can't see that this is my problem.

SKEFFINGTON

It's everyone's problem if an innocent man's been wronged!

GETLIFFE

But that has yet to be established, hasn't it?

(*With a sudden jocular heartiness*)

Look here, Julian, my advice to you is to get together with Nightingale and see if one of you can't change the other's mind. By far the best thing would be for the two of you to produce a combined report. Then I'm sure all the rest of us would accept your recommendation, whether you wanted us to stay put or take some action. The essential thing is that you and Alec should agree.

MARTIN

Do you think it's likely Alec will change his mind?

GETLIFFE

Perhaps Julian will change his.

SKEFFINGTON

You don't seriously think that's on the cards?

GETLIFFE

I don't see why not.

SKEFFINGTON

Why not? Why not? Good God, man—

LEWIS

Look, Francis, why don't you let Julian send you round the evidence—the complete file? Then you can go through it at leisure and make up your mind.

GETLIFFE

No. No, I really can't be involved. If he and Nightingale do a joint report, I'll be glad to study it. I can't go further. I have some new experiments coming out. They're extremely important. They're taking up all my time. I'm sure you understand. Forgive me.

(*He goes quickly out.*)

LEWIS

(*To* SKEFFINGTON)

I told you it was going to be difficult.

SKEFFINGTON

I'm not leaving it at that. Francis—wait. Francis!

(SKEFFINGTON *goes after* GETLIFFE.)

LEWIS

(*Looking after* SKEFFINGTON)

If Howard were in Skeffington's shoes and he were in Howard's—I wonder—would Howard do as much for him?

MARTIN

It's an academic question.

LEWIS

Justice for the enemy? Isn't it the sixty-four-thousand-dollar question? What's Howard's address?

MARTIN

I'm coming with you.

(*As they start for the door*—)


*C U R T A I N*

# ACT TWO

*Scene 2*

*A bed, cheap furniture, provincial ugliness.* HOWARD *stands motionless, staring at the door. He turns slowly, lights a cigarette. His hand is trembling. He slumps on the bed, burying his head in his hands. A door slams off.* LAURA *comes quickly in. She wears a raincoat.*

LAURA

(*At once*)

I saw the Eliots crossing the street. What did they want, Don? What did they—Don!

(HOWARD *is shaking convulsively.*)

My God, what have they done to you?

(*She goes to him, fiercely protective, takes him in her arms, holds him to her, stroking his head.*)

Darling—what have they been saying?

HOWARD

(*Trembling, straightening up*)

Hell. Sorry.

LAURA

The bastards. What happened?

98

HOWARD

Nothing.

LAURA

Tell me.

HOWARD

Nothing. Questions. Over and over and over. Questions.

LAURA

What sort of questions?

HOWARD

It doesn't matter.

LAURA

What questions, Don?

HOWARD

(*Wearily*)

"Have you seen this book?" "Have you seen that page?" "Cast your mind back to when you and Palairet—"

LAURA

Book? What book?

HOWARD

Forget it, will you? Better still—

(*Drawing her to him*)

Help me forget it.

LAURA

*What* page? *What* book?

HOWARD

They've found a notebook.

LAURA
Yours?

HOWARD
Palairet's.

LAURA

(*Eagerly*)

And?

HOWARD
There's a caption under a photograph— Look, Laura, it's unimportant.

LAURA
It can't be or they wouldn't have come. Go on.

HOWARD

(*Wearily*)

The caption and the print together might just possibly clear me, that's all.

LAURA

(*Elated*)

All? That's *all?*

HOWARD
Don't get excited. The photograph's missing.

LAURA
Missing?

HOWARD
Like in communiques—"one of our photographs failed to return." We're back where we started.

LAURA

Then why did they come?

HOWARD

To ask if I'd ever seen the print.

LAURA

And had you?

HOWARD

No.

LAURA

Did you tell them that?

HOWARD

Yes.

LAURA

Why?

HOWARD

Because I hadn't, dear.

LAURA

No one could prove you hadn't.

HOWARD

I know I look like a liar. Do you want me to be one?

LAURA

That was a mistake, Don. You should have sworn you'd seen that photograph.

HOWARD

"The end justifies the means." Unquote.

LAURA

(*Flaring*)

Was what they've done to *you* so honest?

HOWARD

I could not love thee, dear, so much, loved I not honour more. And speaking of love, I'd be grateful—

LAURA

(*Caressing his head*)

Oh, Don, Don, don't you know—don't you *mind* what they've done to you?

HOWARD

It's over now.

LAURA

Over? This thing will follow you for the rest of your life. Apply for a job, there it will be. Ask for a reference, there it will be—round your neck like a leper's bell. They've put you on permanent probation. For what? Daring to hold a vision of life that happens to be unpopular with a pack of over-civilised academics, swilling their port and snoring in Chapel. My God, who's more useful to society, you or them?

HOWARD

It depends which society you're talking about. They are—to theirs.

LAURA

I'm talking about—

HOWARD

Don't. Don't talk. Come to bed.

LAURA

What else did they say?

HOWARD
Who?

LAURA
The Eliots.

HOWARD
I don't remember. Come to—

LAURA
For God's sake, Don. This is our future.

HOWARD

(*Wearily*)

What else did they say—? Let me see. Oh, yes. They're trying to get
a majority. It's a waste of time.

LAURA
Did you tell them that too?

HOWARD
They wouldn't have listened. Once a thing like this gets going, once
you become an excuse for other people's morality, they don't thank
you to pour cold water. The fine words fly—the noble sentiments—
everyone basks in a golden glow. Everyone except the object of the
exercise, who shudders into the nearest corner and tries to stop
shaking.

(*He is trembling again.*)

LAURA

(*Quickly*)

I'll make tea.

HOWARD

(*At once*)

No. Stay with me.

LAURA

(*Comforting him*)

It's a mood, darling. It'll pass. I get them.

HOWARD

You? Never. Strong—masterful—self-sufficient—that's my Laura.

LAURA

So that's how you see me. Do you know my private nightmare? Life without you. Illness—an accident—some other woman—

HOWARD

No other woman. . . .

(*He seizes her and embraces her fiercely. For a moment she yields and they are locked together on the bed. She breaks.*)

LAURA

No. No, I want to think.

HOWARD

And I want not to. I want *not* to think, Laura.

LAURA

(*Planning aloud*)

A majority. Let's see. We'll have the Court against us, naturally. That's Brown, Winslow, Nightingale—

HOWARD

(*From the bed, pleading*)

Laura, please—

LAURA

One or two others, such as Gay because he's too old and the Master because he's technically neutral, won't vote either way—

HOWARD

Laura—

LAURA

That's equivalent to voting against. Then there's that idiot Lester Ince. Tom Orbell's vote will cancel his—

HOWARD

It won't.

LAURA

(*Surprised*)

Tom? He's with us.

HOWARD

No.

LAURA

But I thought—

HOWARD

No. The Eliots say no.

LAURA

Daren't stand up to the brass when it comes to it. I should have guessed. What about Getliffe? What about that fine progressive, Sir Francis?

HOWARD

Neutral. What is equivalent to *et cetera.*

LAURA

It's not going to be easy. Who have we got?

HOWARD

So far, Skeffington.

LAURA

Skeffington?

HOWARD

Yes, the Pope is with us. Also Martin, Taylor, Harris, Parker.

LAURA

Five. We need—what?

HOWARD

Ten. We'll never make it.

LAURA

We'll make it. If I have to march into the Senate House, we'll make it.

(*Suddenly*)

Don, I've just thought—that missing print—

HOWARD

(*Abruptly*)

Forget it. I'm not going on.

LAURA

Perhaps it's no accident it's missing.

HOWARD

I've had enough. I'm going to chuck it.

LAURA

Perhaps the people who wanted to get rid of you found it convenient to get rid of the photograph!

HOWARD

(*Violently*)

Listen to me! I can't take it again. It's finished. I can't go through it a fourth time.

LAURA

(*Grimly*)

We're not giving up now.

HOWARD

Laura, please—I'm tired sick—

LAURA

Do you think I'm not? I've fought this thing for you—with you. Do you think it's easy for *me?*

HOWARD

You don't get taken apart in public. For you it's a moral crusade. You go angrily to sleep—but you sleep. I lie awake, sweating, knowing I'm going to look like a fool and sound like a liar and make the usual foul impression. It's not worth the candle. To hell with it. All right, they win—let them. I'm sick of grubbing about in the gutter. I'm through, I tell you, I'm through!

LAURA

(*Staring*)

What's happened to you?

HOWARD

I've run out of steam, that's what happened. The battle's over. Sue for terms. No, don't. Who cares? Unconditional surrender.

LAURA

You bloody little coward.

(*He stares at her. She turns away. There is a pause.*)

HOWARD

(*Quietly*)

How do you know I didn't do it? Laura? How do you know I didn't do—exactly what they said I did?

(*She turns slowly and looks at him.*)

LAURA

Because you're you.

HOWARD

And you take me on trust.

LAURA

Of course.

HOWARD

Bravely spoken. Why?

LAURA

What else can I do?

HOWARD

That's right. You're not a scientist. So you don't *know*, do you? You *can't* know, can you? Suppose I've been having you on a string?

LAURA

I see. Now it's *my* turn to be punished.

HOWARD

Suppose I said, "Listen, it happened just the way they said, I'm in this up to the neck?"

LAURA

You could say it. I wouldn't believe it.

HOWARD

Not even if it eased my conscience? After all, I have a motive. I was never Alpha plus—I needed that photograph. —Well? Why don't you ask me? Say, "By the way, dear, purely as a matter of interest, did you do it? Are you a fake?" You must have thought it sometime, somewhere. So go on, say it.

LAURA

(*Blazing*)

All right, all *right! Are you a fake?*

(*Pause*)

HOWARD

Would it make a difference to *us*, if I was? Principles—hopes—all down the drain. Would it make a difference?

(*Pause*)

(*Her arms go round him. They cling together.*)

LAURA

Don't do that to me ever again. You frightened me.

(*He laughs.*)

Say you'll go on!

HOWARD

I'm a rotten witness. I can't seem to make the right noises, or faces. I'm bad with people.

LAURA

(*A whisper*)

You're good with me.

(*They kiss.*)

You're good with me. Say you'll go on, *please*.

HOWARD

You get a vein—just there—when you're excited. I noticed it the first time I saw you—at that C.P.U. meeting in Holborn—remember?

LAURA

I remember *you* at that meeting—on the platform. The things you said—the way you said them—you *cared*. You really cared. Do you *still* care, Don?

HOWARD

I care—for you. I care—very much—for you.

LAURA

(*Tense*)

Then fight this—for me!

(*He looks at her curiously.*)

HOWARD

You want to win, don't you? You want it passionately.

LAURA

(*Fiercely*)

Yes! Yes! Yes!

HOWARD

Why?

LAURA

(*Flushed with excitement*)

I want to beat the dynosaurs. I want to rub those civilised snouts in the dust. I want to stand on the roof of their big fat Chapel and shout, "There's a new world coming up—and it's ours, not yours! You're dead! You're yesterday! We're tomorrow! Move over!"

HOWARD

(*Affectionately*)

Intolerant little Utopian.

LAURA

We can't afford tolerance.

HOWARD

What about justice, Laura? Can't we afford justice?

LAURA

Who for? The enemy? Don't be sentimental.

HOWARD

Strong, masterful, self-sufficient—that's my Laura.

LAURA

(*Suddenly*)

No! No, I need *you!* In every possible way, I need you!

(*He stares at her, puzzled.*)

HOWARD

I'm here.

(*He draws her to him on the bed as—*)


T H E   C U R T A I N   F A L L S .

## ACT TWO

*Scene 3*

THE COMBINATION ROOM. EVENING

*The after-dinner wine is laid out. The windows onto the terrace are open.* INCE, NIGHTINGALE *and* BROWN *are standing, taking wine together.* SKEFFINGTON *stands apart at the windows, staring out.*

INCE

But where's all the money coming from? You're not serious, Bursar?

NIGHTINGALE

Indeed I am. It's going to be a fine building. Another eighty sets of rooms.

INCE

But that'll cost the College a quarter of a million.

BROWN

We mean to do the young gentlemen well.

NIGHTINGALE

A few more bequests like Professor Palairet's and we shall soon reach our target figure.

(WINSLOW *comes in.*)

INCE

In that case, here's to old Professor Palairet. May his shadow never grow less.

112

WINSLOW

From the look of this communication there seems little danger of that.

(*He hands a note to* INCE *and sits down, watching the effect on the others with relish.* INCE *reads:*

INCE

"Confidential. To all Fellows. After further study of the new evidence relating to the thesis and publications of D. C. Howard and the notebooks of the late C. J. B. Palairet, F. R. S., I have come to the conclusion that Dr. Skeffington is right in representing that there is a case to answer. I think it is urgent that the College should request the Court of Seniors to consider this case without delay. Signed: F. E. Getliffe."

(*A stunned silence. Then:*)

NIGHTINGALE

Getliffe!

BROWN

But I was given to understand—

WINSLOW

I, too. It would appear that our distinguished colleague has changed his mind.

INCE

Or had it changed for him.

WINSLOW

In either event, a remarkable display of flexibility. What do you say, Senior Tutor?

BROWN

I think Getliffe has been most ill-advised.

NIGHTINGALE

Hear, hear.

SKEFFINGTON

(*Suddenly*)

On the contrary, he deserves a blazing vote of thanks.

BROWN

One hardly thanks a man for putting a pistol to one's head.

NIGHTINGALE

Some of us are not all that fond of being threatened.

SKEFFINGTON

Since when has justice been a threat—except to a man with a guilty conscience?

BROWN

Are you suggesting—?

SKEFFINGTON

Yes, by God, I am! It's not important to be fair. All that matters is that everything should *look* fair!

BROWN

I'm not taking that from you, Julian—

NIGHTINGALE

No, nor am I. Either you withdraw—

SKEFFINGTON

I'm not withdrawing!

WINSLOW

Gentlemen, gentlemen—

INCE

The rain it falleth on the just and on the unjust Fellows—

SKEFFINGTON

That's right! Laugh! Make everything a joke!

INCE

(TOM ORBELL *comes in from the hall, followed by* LEWIS *and* MARTIN.)

TOM

No, Lewis. I'm sorry. It's out of the question.

LEWIS

Won't you talk it over on the plane of reason? Preferably with Martin?

TOM

I haven't the least desire to talk to Martin. I shall only hear what you've just said, ten times worse.

MARTIN

This is vital, Tom. We need two more votes for a majority. Just two votes.

LEWIS

Stand up and be counted, man.

TOM

I can't afford the consequences.

MARTIN

Damn the consequences.

TOM

There are times when one has to consider oneself. You're not making yourselves popular by what you're doing.

MARTIN

And you're not behaving up to your usual standard.

LEWIS
May I remind you that you got me into this?

TOM
I hope you're not saying I forced your hand?

LEWIS
I'm reminding you of your responsibility.

TOM
I have no responsibility. I'm not involved.

LEWIS
I think so.

TOM

(*Stiffly*)

I'm sorry we don't see eye to eye. I mean that, both of you, very sincerely.

(*He turns away to* NIGHTINGALE *and* BROWN. *They turn instinctively to* INCE.)

LEWIS
Lester—?

INCE

(*At once*)

Oh no, Lew. I'm not playing. So far as I'm concerned, this is a squabble among scientists.

MARTIN
That's just letting yourself out. I'm telling you you can't.

INCE
And I'm telling you—can't I hell?

LEWIS

Look, you must admit there's a chance, we think it's a near-certainty, that an innocent man has been victimised.

INCE

Oh, if that sort of thing happens, it always comes out all right in the wash.

LEWIS

Good God above, that's about the most optimistic statement on human affairs that I've ever heard.

INCE

How many people have you seen done down in your time?

LEWIS

Quite a lot, but not quite—

INCE

Then why the sweet hell don't you go and put *that* right?

LEWIS

I was going to say not quite in this way. And just because a lot of people are done down inevitably, that's no reason to add another.

INCE

If you really want to know why I wash my hands of this schemozzle, there's too much Pecksniffery about it. You scientists think you can do anything you like with the world and switch on the moral uplift when you want to feel good. Well, I'm bleeding-well not playing. You go and do good, I shan't get in your way. But I don't want to hear about it. You sort it out among yourselves, and good luck to you and a nice long good-bye kiss.

(*He goes out to the terrace.*)

BROWN

(*Motioning* LEWIS *aside*)

Lewis, old friend.

LEWIS

(*Crossing to* BROWN)

Arthur?

BROWN

I'm going to ask you a personal favour.

LEWIS

Yes, Arthur?

BROWN

Drop this business.

LEWIS

I can't do that, Arthur, not even for you.

BROWN

For the sake of the College.

LEWIS

We must get the right answer.

BROWN

We have it already.

LEWIS

No.

BROWN

I hate to see us on opposite sides.

LEWIS

I don't like that either.

(*A commotion is heard off.*)

NEWBY

(*Off*)

Can you see the step, sir?

GAY

(*Off*)

Of course I can see the step. Do you think I'm blind?

WINSLOW

Dear God, spring has arrived.

(GAY *hobbles urgently in from the hall. Muffled and coated against the night air, he is supported on either side by* NEWBY *and an* ASSISTANT PORTER. *He is in a state of high excitement.*)

GAY

Is young Eliot here? Where's young Eliot? Ah, there you are, my dear chap!

(*To the* PORTERS)

Stand by, men, this will only take a moment. I haven't come here to make conversation. I have just received a remarkable communication.

(*He produces a copy of* GETLIFFE's *note.*)

"To all Fellows." Yes, indeed.

(*To* LEWIS)

Pray tell me, Eliot, you're a lawyer—who is the Senior Fellow of this College?

LEWIS

Why, you are, of course.

GAY

Indeed I am, indeed I am. So no doubt it will surprise you to learn that when the Court of Seniors met last year—over this little trouble of Getliffe's, I presume, but that's neither here nor there—when the

Court met, I was not invited to take my rightful place. Not only was I not invited, I was treated as though I were no longer *compos mentis!*

BROWN

I assure you we had no intention—

GAY

Yes, you did. You had every intention. I had letters, Eliot, from the Master, implying that it might be too much for me. Letters full of fine sentiments, but fine words butter no parsnips. Tell me, am I or am I not entitled to sit on the Court of Seniors, unless I withdraw of my own free will?

LEWIS

I must look up the Statutes.

GAY

Tell me, did they or did they not deprive me of my place without my consent?

BROWN

No, no, no—

GAY

Yes, yes, yes! And if the Court meets again, you'll be at it again! Not letting a man take a place which is his of right—that is a comment on his fitness. So now I deliver my ultimatum. Either the College makes amends—or I sue the College! Sue the College, that's what I'll do! You remember Frederick the Great—there are still judges in Berlin. Well, I believe there is still justice in England. Justice, that's what I want to see—and justice, that's what I mean to have!

LEWIS

Then you are in favour of re-opening the matter?

GAY

What do you advise?

LEWIS

Well, if the Court was not properly constituted . . .

GAY

I take your point. A capital point. Absolutely. Re-open the matter.

LEWIS

Can we count on your vote?

GAY

Certainly you may. Certainly you may.

BROWN

But you know nothing of the issues involved.

GAY

(*With a roar*)

And whose fault was that? The Court was not properly constituted. Very well, the Court must be made to sit again. Let all guns be brought to bear. Count on me, Eliot, I'm your man. What am I—a cypher? And now, men, back to the taxi!

(*He turns, exhausted, and is borne almost bodily out by the* PORTERS.)

BROWN

(*Mopping his brow*)

Winslow, I think we may have to ask you to form a deputation of one to try and dissuade the Senior Fellow.

(WINSLOW *rises and draws himself up with dignity.*)

WINSLOW

I have done a certain amount of service for this College, most of it quite undistinguished in the course of a misspent life. The one service I will not do for this College is to expose myself to the conversation of M. H. L. Gay. It was jejune at the best of times, and now that what by courtesy one refers to as his mind appears to have given up the very unequal struggle, I find it bizarre but unrewarding.

(*With which he goes out.*)

BROWN

In that case, I shall have to tackle him myself, I suppose. Ah—Master.

(THOMAS CRAWFORD, *the Master of the College, has come in from the door leading to the Lodge. He wears a black gown. Those who are seated rise.*)

CRAWFORD

Please don't disturb yourselves. I just wanted to take a few soundings about this fly-sheet of Getliffe's.

(*He produces it from a pocket.*)

I presume you've all seen it.

(*To* LEWIS)

I gather, Eliot, that you're not unfamiliar with this unfortunate business?

LEWIS

No, and I think I should say straight away, Master, that if I were a Fellow now, I should be in favour of re-opening this case, without any qualification at all.

CRAWFORD

You must forgive me, Eliot, but that does sound like a premature judgment.

BROWN

I'm surprised that Lewis feels in a position to make any judgment whatever.

(*To* LEWIS)

Do you think that in reaching our decision we were altogether irresponsible?

LEWIS

I'm not suggesting that for a moment. But would you say Francis Getliffe was a man given to premature judgments?

CRAWFORD

You have a point there. Getliffe is a distinguished man of science—

BROWN

I'm sorry, but I can't accept that as a reason for giving up our responsibility.

CRAWFORD

Of course, I'm in general agreement with you, Senior Tutor.

BROWN

If Getliffe had come to you, Master, about his difficulty, that would have been another matter. But the way he's gone about it, it's making the College into a bear-garden.

CRAWFORD

Yes, one would have thought that Getliffe wouldn't have wished to create unnecessary commotion. One doesn't want fuss in a place like this. One wants quiet and the climate of contemplation. I'll try to have a word with Getliffe next Thursday at the Royal Society.

LEWIS

I think you should know that several others, not only Getliffe, are of the opinion that there is a case for enquiry.

BROWN

Of course, if there's a majority for re-opening the case, then by the Statutes the Seniors naturally have to do so. But frankly, I don't see that happening.

LEWIS

I think Martin has something to say about that.

MARTIN

I don't want to do too much counting heads, Master, but nine out of nineteen feel the other way.

CRAWFORD

Is that a firm figure?

MARTIN

Yes, there are nine Fellows willing to vote for re-opening. We are just one short of a majority.

BROWN

I accept Martin's figures. But—

NIGHTINGALE

Yes. But I'm sure he would agree that the nine he's referred to do not include, apart from Getliffe and himself, any of our more influential members.

MARTIN

That's true, but surely it's the numbers themselves that—

CRAWFORD

(*Topping everyone*)

Speaking as Master, there is one point I should like to stress. The more we ventilate this matter internally, the greater the risk of an outside leak. I'm not sure that to continue raking over dead ashes might not be tempting Providence too far. How do you feel, Bursar?

NIGHTINGALE

I have always regretted that I was party to Howard's election. I know politics is almost a taboo word, but, frankly, I am not convinced that a man of his political colour can be a man of good character, as I understand the term. And I am not prepared to welcome such men in the name of tolerance, the tolerance they themselves despise.

SKEFFINGTON

(*Who has come in from the terrace just before* NIGHTINGALE's *speech*)

That's a perfectly monstrous thing to say. He's entitled to justice the same as the next man. The Seniors have made a crashing mistake.

BROWN

I'm sorry. We're all human and liable to err, but I've seldom been more certain I was right.

SKEFFINGTON

Then it's time we had someone unprejudiced on this wretched Court!

NIGHTINGALE

Are you suggesting we should give up our places on the Court of Seniors simply because we don't find ourselves able to accept your judgment?

SKEFFINGTON

No. Because you won't admit the facts when you see them.

NIGHTINGALE

I don't accept your interpretation of them.

SKEFFINGTON

And Getliffe's?

NIGHTINGALE

Yes, I suppose we have you to thank for Getliffe's defection.

CRAWFORD

I think perhaps we had better leave this for tonight.

SKEFFINGTON

No, Master. I'm not going to have this man left with a black mark against him while you put us off with one sidestep after another. If you can't give us a decent constitutional method of getting a bit of simple justice, then we shall have to try something else.

CRAWFORD

I'm not clear what else you can try.

SKEFFINGTON

I can make the whole case public.

BROWN
What?

SKEFFINGTON
I don't like it. It won't do me any good, or the College. But it will do some good to the one chap who most needs it. The minute we let a breath of fresh air into this business, you won't have a leg to stand on.

CRAWFORD
Are you saying that you're prepared to get the College into the papers?

SKEFFINGTON
Certainly I am.

CRAWFORD
I'm obliged to tell you that I'm astonished to hear the bare suggestion.

NIGHTINGALE
I hope you realise, Skeffington, how unforgivable all of us here would judge any such action to be.

SKEFFINGTON
I repeat, unless someone can think up a nicer way, I'm ready to blow the whole thing wide open.

   (*Pause*)

BROWN
I should be surprised if you didn't think better of it.

   (*Pause*)

SKEFFINGTON
I shan't.

   (*He goes out. A silence. Then* CRAWFORD *turns deliberately to* NIGHTINGALE.)

CRAWFORD

Which architect had you in mind for your new building, Bursar—
or is that a premature question?

NIGHTINGALE

No, indeed. I've been giving the matter some thought and I've come
to the conclusion that perhaps we should select two orthodox men
and two modernists and invite all four to submit plans.

CRAWFORD

Two of each school. Yes, that seems equitable. Then no one can
accuse us of turning our backs on the past or rushing headlong into
the future.

BROWN

A glass of port, Master?

CRAWFORD

That would be very agreeable, Senior Tutor, but I was about to
suggest that you and the Bursar take wine with me in the Lodge,
and then perhaps we could continue our little discussion in private.
That is, if you can spare me five minutes?

BROWN

Of course, Master.

NIGHTINGALE

Certainly, Master.

CRAWFORD

(*To* NIGHTINGALE *as they go*)

I agree entirely, we should set our sights high. Comfort without lux-
ury, elegance without ostentation. We want to leave behind us
something not only the College but the University can look on with
pride in the years to come.

(*Followed by* BROWN *and* NIGHTINGALE, CRAWFORD *passes with dignity into the Lodge.*)

(*Apart from the* ELIOTS, *there is no one left in the room but* TOM ORBELL.)

TOM

(*Quietly, staring at the door to the Lodge*)

God rot them. Got rot those awful old men and their deadly dehydrated souls. Lord knows I don't like Howard, but was one word said, was one word even thought about the man himself? Unnecessary commotion! Raking over dead ashes! It was so dehumanised, I could vomit. I'll come in with you, by God I will!

MARTIN

Do you mean it?

TOM

Do you think it's easy for me to say? Here, give me your hand.

(*He grasps* MARTIN'S *hand.*)

LEWIS

(*At the table, writing something*)

I wonder if you'd mind putting it in writing?

TOM

(*Stung*)

You want it on paper, do you? All right.

(LEWIS *passes him the note. He scribbles his signature, hands the note defiantly to* LEWIS.)

There's your blasted majority!

*CURTAIN*

# ACT THREE

# ACT THREE

*Scene 1*

*The College bell is tolling.* NEWBY, *the head porter, his bowler hat on, is putting the final touches to the room, which has been arranged to form the Court of Seniors.*

*Four chairs, are set along one side of the long rosewood table. Before each chair are a blotter, a pile of quarto paper, a pen and pencils. Also on the table are the College Statutes, a collection of Palairet's notebooks, a slimmer, green book, also with gold lettering, three water jugs and some glasses.*

*On the left side of the room, facing inward, are two elegant desks and chairs, each identically equipped with blotter, pen, pencils, water jug and glass. On the right side of the room, opposite, is a single chair. The sun is streaming in through the windows.*

LEWIS *strides briskly in. He wears an M.A.'s gown and hood and carries a briefcase. He goes straight to the desk on the left.*

LEWIS
Morning, Newby.

NEWBY
Good morning, sir. Lovely day, sir.

LEWIS
Yes, it's good to see the sun.

(*He opens the briefcase and takes out some papers.*)

NEWBY

I think you'll find everything you need, sir.

LEWIS

Oh. Yes. Thanks.

NEWBY

A bit like sitting for the Tripos, sir.

LEWIS

Yes—and I'm still not sure I know the answers.

(DAWSON-HILL *enters. Elegant, sleekly immaculate,* DAWSON-HILL *is a year* LEWIS'S *senior. He is similarly gowned and carries a briefcase.*)

NEWBY

Mr. Dawson-Hill, sir.

DAWSON-HILL

Newby!

NEWBY

Good to see you back, sir.

DAWSON-HILL

(*Warmly*)

This is like old times.

(*Shaking hands*)

You haven't changed a muscle.

NEWBY

Don't know about that, sir. You're looking well, sir.

DAWSON-HILL

And my dear Lewis!

(*Strides across and shakes hands*)

How extremely nice to see you!

LEWIS

Good morning.

(*Indicating desk*)

I've pinched this one. All right?

DAWSON-HILL

(*Amused*)

Left of centre. But of course, my dear Lewis, of course.

(*He goes to the downstage desk, opens his briefcase and takes out papers.*)

NEWBY

I was wondering, gentlemen. About the glare. Should I pull a blind?

LEWIS

Not for me. The more light the better.

DAWSON-HILL

Hear, hear.

NEWBY

Right, sir. Thank you, sir.

(*He goes out.*)

(*The bell stops tolling. The College clock begins to chime ten. Almost at once the door to the Lodge opens and the Seniors enter,* CRAWFORD *first, followed by* BROWN, WINSLOW *and* NIGHT-INGALE, *who carries a ledger, and finally* PROFESSOR GAY *in a wheelchair, propelled by a bowler-hatted* ASSISTANT PORTER.
*All are capped and gowned, and wearing the full regalia of their University degrees and offices, the* MASTER *in his red robes.* GAY *wears an ancient gown over his topcoat, with a muffler at his throat and an old-fashioned wide-brimmed homberg perched on his head. The procession divides,* CRAWFORD *taking the centre chair, with* GAY *in his wheelchair on his immediate left,* WINSLOW *on* CRAWFORD'S *right, and* NIGHTINGALE *on* GAY'S *left,* BROWN *on* WINSLOW'S *right. They seat themselves.*)

*During the scene that follows,* NIGHTINGALE, *as Secretary of the Court, takes full notes of the proceedings. The other members take notes occasionally.)*

CRAWFORD

(*To* LEWIS *and* DAWSON-HILL)

Good morning, gentlemen.

LEWIS ⎫
DAWSON-HILL ⎭
Good morning, Master.

GAY

I trust no one objects if I keep my hat on. To avoid the draughts, you understand.

CRAWFORD
Not at all, Moderator.

GAY

Ah, Moderator. I like that term. That's a term and a half!

(*To* CRAWFORD)

Tell me, my dear chap, what is your name?

CRAWFORD

(*Astonished*)

I am Thomas Crawford, Master of the College.

GAY
I congratulate you.

CRAWFORD
Perhaps I ought to introduce my colleagues—

GAY

Quite unnecessary, my dear chap. Just because one has a slip of memory with your face, it doesn't mean that one forgets the others. Good morning. Good morning. Good morning.

("*Good mornings*" *are returned along the table, as* GAY *nods to each of the others in turn.*)

CRAWFORD

In any case, I expect you don't remember our legal advisers here. May I present—?

GAY

Quite unnecessary once more. This is Sir Lewis Eliot, K.B.E., M.A., who is to represent young Howard. A former Fellow of the College, he went out of residence during the war, and then subsequently did service for the State which has been publicly recognised. Hobbies: tennis and chess. And this must be Dawson-Hill, M.A., Q.C., who is to represent the Court. One time scholar of the College, eminent lawyer, member of the Athenaeum and Pratts. Hobbies: fencing and fishing. You see, I've done my homework, my dear ——? I do apologise, but your name obstinately escapes me.

CRAWFORD

Crawford.

GAY

Ah, yes. Our present Master. I'd better call you Master. I've done my homework, you see—Master. *Who's Who*, that's a fine book. That's a book and a half.

WINSLOW

I confess I'm not quite clear about the purpose of these preliminaries—

GAY

Aren't you, my dear chap? I am perfectly clear. But thank you for reminding me of my office. Gentlemen, I am about to give you your marching orders.

BROWN

Do you wish us to stand?

GAY

No, no, don't exhaust yourselves.

(*He takes a sheet of paper from his pocket and studies it through a large magnifying glass.*)

As Moderator in the present proceedings before the Court of Seniors, I must request Eliot and Dawson-Hill to pay special attention to what I am about to say. The Court of Seniors has recently decided upon the deprivation of a Fellow. That decision has not been received with confidence by a number of Fellows. Whether they would have had more confidence if the Court of Seniors, as by right it should, had had an older head among them—it's not for me to say a wiser one—whether in those altered circumstances the Fellows would have had more confidence, why again it's not for me to say. This isn't the time to cry over spilt milk. I am restored to my rightful place on the Court. Honour is served. I ask no more. And now I have to tell you that I don't intend to sit on the Court.

CRAWFORD

What's that?

GAY

Master, I am a little tired. A tired man is a bad judge. So now I give you my parting words. The details of this affair—why, that's the task you've got to put your minds to. It's a task and a half, I can tell you.

(*He grips the arms of the wheelchair and tries to struggle to his feet.*)

BROWN

No, no, you needn't stand.

GAY

Certainly I shall stand.

(*Assisted by* NIGHTINGALE *on one side and the* PORTER *on the other, he manages to stand more or less upright.*)

I would say this. Be bold. Let no man's feelings stand in your way. Justice is more important than any man's feelings. See to it that justice is done—and not only done, but seen to be done. Now I wish you all success in your task. And I wish you good-bye.

(*He falls back in the wheelchair, exhausted.*)

(NIGHTINGALE *opens the door and the* PORTER *trundles the old man back into the Lodge.* NIGHTINGALE *sits down again.*)

CRAWFORD

(*With relief*)

Well, gentlemen, I think we can begin. I will ask the Bursar, as the Secretary of the Court, to read the last order.

(NIGHTINGALE *opens the ledger and reads:*)

NIGHTINGALE

"A Meeting of the Court of Seniors was held on February 22nd, 1961. Present: the Master, Mr. Winslow, Mr. Brown, Dr. Nightingale. The following order was passed: 'That, in response to the wishes of a majority of the College, the Court of Seniors was prepared to hold a further enquiry into the deprivation of Dr. D. C. Howard, in the presence of legal advisers.'"

CRAWFORD

Thank you, Bursar. Our legal advisers are now sitting with us. I have explained to them that it is for Eliot, representing those not satisfied with the Seniors' previous decision, to show cause why we should consider overruling it. That is, Eliot, we feel the onus is on you to persuade a majority of the Court to reverse or modify their previous judgment. We are now four members. If we are unable to reach unanimity, I shall be compelled to take a vote. I have to tell you that, according to precedents in the Court of Seniors, which as far as we can trace has only met three times this century, whilst the Master as a member of the Court has a vote, he does not possess a casting vote. The only comfort is that, whatever rules one has, sensible men usually reach a sensible conclusion. Eliot, we are ready to hear from you.

(*He sits back.*)

(LEWIS *rises.*)

LEWIS
Dr. Howard, please.

(CRAWFORD *rings a small silver handbell.* NEWBY *enters.*)

CRAWFORD
Dr. Howard, please.

NEWBY
Yes, sir.

(NEWBY *goes out. In a moment,* HOWARD *enters. He looks pale, ill-tempered, glowering. With one hand, he pulls his gown across his chest.*)

CRAWFORD
Good morning. Do sit down.

(HOWARD *stands, as if undecided.*)

Won't you sit down?

(HOWARD *sits in the chair right. He is at his worst, and knows it.*)

LEWIS
Doctor Howard, you came up to the College as an undergraduate in 1946?

HOWARD
Yes.

LEWIS
You did your National Service from '48 to '50. You returned to the College in '51 and took Part Two of the Tripos in '53?

HOWARD
Yes.

LEWIS

You then went off to Scotland to do research under Professor Palairet?

HOWARD

Yes.

LEWIS

When you arrived in his laboratory, who suggested your actual field of work?

HOWARD

I don't remember.

LEWIS

Did you suggest it yourself?

HOWARD

I suppose not.

LEWIS

Well then, did Palairet?

HOWARD

I suppose so.

LEWIS

In fact, he laid down your line of research in detail, didn't he, and supervised it day by day?

HOWARD

Yes.

LEWIS

More than a professor normally would?

HOWARD

Maybe.

LEWIS

He was in and out of your room almost daily, wasn't he?

HOWARD

I dare say.

(*Pause*)

(LEWIS *is finding* HOWARD'S *remote and suspicious attitude hard to handle.*)

LEWIS

Did you find research easy?

HOWARD

I shouldn't think anyone ever does.

LEWIS

Some of the results you obtained under Professor Palairet are still perfectly valid, aren't they?

HOWARD

(*After a pause*)

No one's criticised them yet.

LEWIS

But there was one photograph which was, beyond any doubt, a fraud?

(HOWARD *nods.*)

Can you tell the Court how that photograph got into the experimental data?

(*Pause*)

HOWARD

Palairet must have brought it in.

LEWIS

Can you remember how or when?

HOWARD
No, I can't.

LEWIS
Will you try?

(*Pause*)

HOWARD
No, I can't place it. There were a lot of photographs—I was trying
to write my thesis and explain them.

LEWIS
But this was a more striking bit of experimental evidence than the
rest, wasn't it?

HOWARD
Of course it was.

LEWIS
And you can't remember Palairet first showing it to you?

HOWARD
No, I can't.

(*Pause*)

LEWIS
Was the discovery of the fraud a major shock?

HOWARD
Yes.

LEWIS
When you were first accused, you denied that there was any fraud.
Why did you do that?

HOWARD
It had never crossed my mind.

LEWIS

Quite. It didn't occur to you to think, much less to say, that a man of Palairet's eminence could have done such a thing?

HOWARD

No.

LEWIS

It was only later, when you were forced to recognise that there had been a fraud, that you realised only one person could have done it?

HOWARD

Yes.

LEWIS

And so that was why, belatedly, so belatedly that it seemed like an invention to save your own skin, you brought in the name of Professor Palairet?

HOWARD

Yes.

LEWIS

Thank you, Doctor Howard.

(LEWIS *sits down.*)

CRAWFORD

Dawson-Hill.

(DAWSON-HILL *rises and goes up to the table at which the Court is sitting.*)

DAWSON-HILL

(*To* NIGHTINGALE)

May I have the thesis, please?

(NIGHTINGALE *hands him the slim green book with* HOWARD'S *name in gold letters on the cover.*)

(DAWSON-HILL *crosses to* HOWARD.)

DAWSON-HILL
This does seem to be your thesis, doesn't it, Doctor Howard?

HOWARD
Of course.

DAWSON-HILL
How many copies are there in existence?

HOWARD
Four.

DAWSON-HILL
Where are they?

HOWARD
The College has two. I used the other two for other applications.

DAWSON-HILL
This is the show copy?

HOWARD
You can call it that.

(*A slip of paper protrudes from the thesis.*)
(DAWSON-HILL *opens it at that page.*)

DAWSON-HILL
Then this would be your star print?

(*He holds up the photograph—concentric rings of black and grey, not unlike an archery target.*)

HOWARD
It's a print all right.

DAWSON-HILL

And this print is a fraud?

(*Pause*)

HOWARD

Yes.

DAWSON-HILL

That doesn't need proving, does it? All the scientific opinion agrees that the drawing-pin hole is expanded? Isn't that true?

HOWARD

I suppose so.

DAWSON-HILL

That is, this print has been expanded to make it look like something it's not?

HOWARD

I suppose so.

DAWSON-HILL

What about your other prints?

HOWARD

Which other prints?

DAWSON-HILL

You can't misunderstand me, Doctor Howard. The prints in the other copies of your thesis.

HOWARD

I think I re-photographed them from this one.

DAWSON-HILL

You *think?*

HOWARD

I must have done.

DAWSON-HILL

And this one—this fake—came from a negative which you never produced? Where is it, do you know?

HOWARD

Of course I don't. I never saw it. Palairet must have made the print and the measurements. I just took them over.

NIGHTINGALE

You mean to say that you used this print as experimental evidence without having the negative in your hands?

HOWARD

I thought the print and the measurements were good enough.

LEWIS

That is, you took them on Palairet's authority?

HOWARD

Yes.

NIGHTINGALE

I'm sorry, I can't imagine anyone doing research like that.

BROWN

I must say, neither can I.

DAWSON-HILL

Doctor Howard, I'm not a scientist, but I believe this particular print was regarded—before it was exposed as a fraud—as the most interesting feature of the thesis?

HOWARD

It was *an* interesting feature.

DAWSON-HILL

Let me be crude. Without that print, and the argument it was supposed to prove, do you believe that the thesis would have won you a Fellowship?

HOWARD

I don't know.

DAWSON-HILL

Do you agree it couldn't have stood the slightest chance?

HOWARD

I shouldn't say that.

BROWN

I understand there's not a great deal of substance in the first half, isn't that so?

(NIGHTINGALE *nods agreement.*)

HOWARD

(*Leafing through the thesis*)

There are these experiments—

NIGHTINGALE

I shouldn't have thought that was very original work, by Fellowship standards.

HOWARD

It's useful. Useful.

DAWSON

At any rate, you'd be prepared to agree that without this somewhat providential photograph your chances could hardly have been called rosy?

(*No reply*)

I wonder if you'd mind giving us some illumination on a slightly different matter. This incident has somewhat, shall I say, disarranged your career?

HOWARD
What do you think?

DAWSON-HILL
Not to put too fine a point upon it, it's meant that you have had to say good-bye to being a research scientist and start again? Or is that putting it too high?

HOWARD
That's about the size of it.

DAWSON-HILL
You must have realized that would ensue as soon as this Court deprived you of your Fellowship?

HOWARD
Well, of course I did.

DAWSON-HILL
That was, let me see, just over a year ago?

HOWARD

(*Savagely*)

You must have the date.

DAWSON-HILL
And yet during that time, that quite appreciable time, you never took any legal action?

HOWARD
No.

DAWSON-HILL

You've never been to see your Solicitor?

HOWARD

Not as far as I can remember.

DAWSON-HILL

You must remember. Have you been or not?

HOWARD

No.

DAWSON-HILL

You never contemplated bringing an action for wrongful dismissal?

HOWARD

No.

DAWSON-HILL

I suggest you weren't willing to face a Court of Law.

HOWARD

I always thought the College would give me a square deal.

DAWSON-HILL

You thought they might give you much more of the benefit of the doubt, wasn't that it?

HOWARD

I tell you, I didn't want to drag the College through the courts!

DAWSON-HILL

Surely that would be more magnanimous than any of us could conceive of being in the circumstances?

HOWARD

I didn't want to drag the College through the courts.

DAWSON-HILL

Forgive me, but have you really this extreme respect for institutions? I rather gathered that you had slightly less respect than most of us?

HOWARD

(*With spirit*)

I've got less respect for existing society than most of you have, if that's what you mean. It's dying on its feet, and none of you realize how fast it's dying. But that doesn't mean I haven't got respect for some institutions inside it. I can see this University going on, and this College, for that matter, long after the system you're all trying to prop up is sunk without trace, except for a few jeers in the history books!

(*A murmur from the Court*)

DAWSON-HILL

Doctor Howard, your interesting attitude toward what I think you called "existing society" brings me to another question. What were your relations with Professor Palairet?

HOWARD

All right.

DAWSON-HILL

You've given the impression that they were slightly closer than one would naturally expect between a very senior professor and, forgive me, a not yet remarkable research student. The impression you've tried to give us is of someone coming in and out of your room, giving you pieces of experimental data, and so on, very much as though he were a collaborator of your own standing. Does that sound likely?

HOWARD

It's what happened.

DAWSON-HILL

Didn't you give Professor Palairet grounds for being less, not more, intimate with you than with other research students?

HOWARD

I don't know what you mean.

DAWSON-HILL

It's common knowledge that Professor Palairet was a very conservative man?

HOWARD

He was a conservative, yes.

DAWSON-HILL

Surely, actively so?

HOWARD

If you put it that way.

DAWSON-HILL

Didn't he ask you to stop your open political activities while you were in his laboratory?

HOWARD

He said something of the sort.

DAWSON-HILL

What did you say?

HOWARD

I said I couldn't.

DAWSON-HILL

Didn't he object when you appeared as one of the backers of what
I believe is called a "Front" organization? "Scientists' World Peace
Conference."—Wasn't that the eloquent name?

HOWARD

I suppose he did.

DAWSON-HILL

Didn't he give you an ultimatum that if you appeared in any such
organization again you would have to leave his laboratory?

HOWARD

I shouldn't have called it an ultimatum.

DAWSON-HILL

But that is substantially true?

HOWARD

There's something in it.

DAWSON-HILL

Well then, does all this correspond to the picture, the rather touching picture I must say, of professor-student intimacy, on which your
whole account of these incidents depends?

(*No answer*)

I suggest to you that, whichever way one looks at it, your story
doesn't make sense. If we assume, just for an instant, that the eminent Professor Palairet did perpetrate a ridiculous fraud, and we also
assume the reality of this touching picture of professor-student intimacy, then we have to accept that he gave you some experimental
data and you quietly put them into your thesis as your own?

HOWARD

I made acknowledgments in everything I wrote.

DAWSON-HILL

But it would mean that you were living on his work?

HOWARD

All the interpretations were mine.

DAWSON-HILL

Does it sound likely behaviour on Professor Palairet's part?

HOWARD

It's what happened! It's what happened!

DAWSON-HILL

Thank you, Master. I've nothing more to ask Doctor Howard.

(DAWSON-HILL *sits down*.)

CRAWFORD

The Court has had opportunity to question Howard on previous occasions. I don't know whether any Senior wishes to ask him anything further now?

WINSLOW

I regard that, Master, as a question asked with the particle "num."

CRAWFORD

What about you, Eliot?

LEWIS

(*Rising, to* HOWARD)

Look here, there's been a fraud. You didn't do it?

HOWARD

No.

LEWIS

In your view it must have been done by Palairet?

HOWARD

I suppose so.

LEWIS

Of anything connected with this fraud you are quite innocent?

HOWARD

(*In a high, strangulated tone*)

But of course I am!

LEWIS

Thank you, Doctor Howard.

(*He sits down.*)

CRAWFORD

Thank you, Howard.

(HOWARD *sits motionless.*)

Thank you. That is all.

(HOWARD *suddenly gets up and goes quickly out.*)
(*The Seniors murmur among themselves.* LEWIS *takes a glass of water*)

LEWIS

Sir Francis Getliffe, please.

(CRAWFORD *rings his bell.* NEWBY *enters.*)

CRAWFORD

Sir Francis Getliffe, please.

NEWBY

Yes, sir.

(NEWBY *goes out.* GETLIFFE *enters. He wears a red robe similar to the* MASTER'S. *He bows to the Court.*)

CRAWFORD

We are very sorry to drag you here, Getliffe. Do sit down.

(GETLIFFE *sits in the witness chair.*)

LEWIS

Sir Francis, you are familiar with the details of the matter before the Court?

GETLIFFE

I am.

LEWIS

When you first heard criticism of Doctor Howard's work from the American laboratories, you took it for granted that Howard himself had faked the photographs in his paper?

GETLIFFE

Certainly.

LEWIS

Accordingly, you accepted the verdict of the Court of Seniors when they first deprived him?

GETLIFFE

In any circumstances I should want very strong reasons not to accept the verdict of the Court of Seniors of this College. In these circumstances I thought their verdict inevitable.

LEWIS

When did you begin to think otherwise?

(*Pause*)

GETLIFFE

Later than I should have done, I'm ashamed to say.

LEWIS

You began to think a mistake might have been made?

GETLIFFE

I should like to be clear about the word "mistake."

LEWIS

Yes?

GETLIFFE

(*Carefully*)

I do not say it was, but I do say most seriously that it may have been worse than a mistake.

CRAWFORD

(*After a moment*)

I'm not sure that I follow you, Getliffe.

LEWIS

Could you elucidate?

GETLIFFE

I believe that throughout this affair Howard has behaved like an innocent and not very intelligent man. I believe his account of what happened is substantially accurate. I believe that most scientists who studied the facts without prejudice would come to the same conclusion.

LEWIS

They would, as a consequence, have to accept that the fraud was done not by Howard but by Palairet?

GETLIFFE

Yes.

CRAWFORD

You're asking us to believe that a man of seventy-two, absolutely established, right at the top of his particular tree, suddenly went in for cooking his results?

GETLIFFE

I am.

CRAWFORD

But what possible motive—?

GETLIFFE

Vanity. A curious kind of vanity. "I have been right so often. I know I'm right this time. This is the way the world was designed. But I'm an old man and my time is short. If the evidence isn't forthcoming, then just for once I'll produce the evidence." Scientists are susceptible to such temptations, you know. I have felt them myself.

WINSLOW

You have not, I trust, succumbed?

GETLIFFE

(*With a smile*)

Not yet.

BROWN

But you maintain that Professor Palairet did?

GETLIFFE

It's the only possible conclusion.

NIGHTINGALE

That is where we fundamentally disagree.

GETLIFFE

How can you? You've only been able to go on persuading yourselves because of one simple fact. If that one photograph were present in Palairet's notebook, not one of you could even pretend to think that he wasn't responsible.

NIGHTINGALE

However, the photograph is not present.

GETLIFFE

That is what I meant by something worse than a mistake.

NIGHTINGALE

If I understand your innuendo correctly—

GETLIFFE

I am not making an innuendo. I am stating a possibility.

LEWIS

And that possibility is—?

GETLIFFE

That the photograph now missing from Palairet's notebook was re-moved *not by accident*, but by someone who wished either to pre-serve Palairet's reputation or to continue justifying the dismissal of Howard.

(*A murmur from the Court*)

BROWN

(*At length*)

That is a very grave thing to say.

GETLIFFE

I know it. I must ask the Court to remember that I have said it.

(DAWSON-HILL *rises.*)

CRAWFORD

Dawson-Hill?

DAWSON-HILL

(*Carefully*)

I think the Court should take note of Sir Francis's extremely interesting conjecture, at the same time bearing in mind that it is only
a conjecture and may well have no basis whatever in fact.

(*He sits down.*)

CRAWFORD

Eliot?

LEWIS

I have no further questions for Sir Francis.

CRAWFORD

Thank you, Getliffe. I think that is all.

(GETLIFFE *rises, bows and goes out.*)
(*Slowly*)

I am inclined to think, gentlemen, that our colleague's . . . conjecture involves us in a certain difficulty. I'm going to ask you to address your minds to the wisest way of removing that difficulty. Eliot,
this development concerns your side of the case. Are you able to give
us a lead?

(LEWIS *rises, but before he can speak:*)

WINSLOW

With your permission, Master.

CRAWFORD

Do you wish to speak now?

WINSLOW

If you please. *If* you please.

(LEWIS *sits down.*)

I may delude myself, but I thought I captured the general drift of what Francis Getliffe was trying to tell us. He appeared to be giving us as his considered opinion that the unfortunate Howard might conceivably have been what I believe is nowadays known as "framed." It seems to me impossible to pretend that Getliffe did not mean what he said. It seems to me *a fortiori* impossible for this Court not to act accordingly. No, I have to correct myself. No doubt nothing is impossible for this Court, or for any other committee of our College. Shall I simply say that it is impossible for me? Indeed, may I bring it to a point?

CRAWFORD

I would be grateful.

WINSLOW

Shortly, my dear Master, your remarkable reign is coming to a close and you will subside into obscurity with the rest of us. In the ensuing election I have never so much as contemplated another candidate than Getliffe. I confess I should find a certain inconsistency in supporting Getliffe for the Mastership and not paying attention to his statement of this morning. I do not propose to exhibit that inconsistency. I should therefore like to give notice, Master, that on this Court I intend to vote for the re-instatement of Howard. I suggest that this is done forthwith. Of course, it will make the Court of Seniors look slightly ridiculous. But then the Court of Seniors *is* slightly ridiculous.

(*He sits back. There is a pause.*)

CRAWFORD

I think we must take note that our Senior colleague has declared his intention.

WINSLOW

If you please, Master. *If* you please.

NIGHTINGALE

I totally disagree with almost everything we heard from Mr. Winslow.

CRAWFORD

(*To* WINSLOW)

So you and the Bursar cancel each other out.

WINSLOW

Very remarkable.

CRAWFORD

Brown?

BROWN

I agree with the Bursar.

WINSLOW

Would it be premature, my dear Master, to enquire your view?

(*Pause*)

CRAWFORD

(*Slowly*)

I do not know that Getliffe convinced me beyond the possibility of doubt that Howard is innocent. He did convince me that it is impossible to say with certainty that he is guilty. I therefore find myself obliged to believe that he should be re-instated by this Court.

WINSLOW

(*With satisfaction*)

I make that *duo utriusque lateris.*

(*To* BROWN)

Two-all.


CRAWFORD

Yes, we are deadlocked. Eliot, I fear you have not persuaded a majority of the Court. Can you help us further?


LEWIS

I think so, Master. I should like to direct the Court's attention to Sir Francis Getliffe's statement.


DAWSON-HILL

(*Rising quickly*)

Master, with apologies to my colleague, I would like to ask if he can see his way to leaving Sir Francis Getliffe's statement as it stands. Naturally, the statement can't be ignored by the Court. But I suggest that if my colleague takes it further we face a prospect of getting into a situation of some delicacy. With great respect, I suggest that we leave it now.


LEWIS

I'm sorry, Master. I can't present a fair case for Howard with one hand tied behind my back.


NIGHTINGALE

(*Suddenly, slamming his hand down hard*)

All right! All right, put your cards on the table. That'd be a change for us all.


LEWIS

(*Calmly*)

If you don't mind, I'd rather put Palairet's notebook on the table.

NIGHTINGALE

(*Furiously*)

I should like a simple answer to a simple question. How much of all this is intended for me?

LEWIS

I don't think the Bursar should conduct my case for me.

NIGHTINGALE

I want to know whether what Getliffe said was intended for me!

LEWIS

May we have the notebook open on the table? Perhaps the Bursar can help me find the place.

(*He opens the notebook and turns the pages.*)

It's somewhere near halfway through. Ah, this is it, isn't it?

NIGHTINGALE

Yes.

LEWIS

There, gentlemen.

(*He lays the open notebook in front of the Court.*)

You heard Getliffe's opinion. He said it was possible that the photograph which used to be on that page had been torn out. *Not by chance.* And now may I ask the Bursar one or two questions?

CRAWFORD

Are you prepared for that, Nightingale?

NIGHTINGALE
Of course.

(*He rises.*)

LEWIS
You need not move.

NIGHTINGALE
I prefer to.

(*He crosses and sits on the witness chair.*)

LEWIS
The notebook arrived at the Bursary on January 5th last. Is that correct?

NIGHTINGALE
Yes.

LEWIS
You were the first person in the College to see it?

NIGHTINGALE
Naturally.

LEWIS
Do you remember when you saw it?

NIGHTINGALE
The day it arrived.

LEWIS
Do you remember this page?

NIGHTINGALE
Not particularly.


LEWIS
Then you can't say if there was a photograph there or not?


NIGHTINGALE
Yes. There must have been.


LEWIS
How can you be sure?


NIGHTINGALE
If there had not been, I should have noticed the blank space.


LEWIS
And there was no blank space?


NIGHTINGALE
None.


LEWIS
Bursar, if there was a photograph there—it must have been a fake, mustn't it?


NIGHTINGALE
Not necessarily.


LEWIS
Oh, come. It has been established that the caption beneath it is un-true—or do you dispute that?

NIGHTINGALE

No, I don't say Palairet's conclusions were right. I agree he must have been mistaken. But the photograph from which he drew those conclusions may very well have been genuine.

LEWIS

*May* have been genuine? Don't you know?

NIGHTINGALE

I can't be certain. I only gave it a cursory glance.

LEWIS

A cursory glance? But you're a scientist. You must have examined the print with care.

NIGHTINGALE

Not at the time. I was too busy.

LEWIS

Too busy?

NIGHTINGALE

Too busy! The Bursarship is an extremely arduous and responsible post and one which I am deeply proud to hold.

LEWIS

And your responsibilities to Doctor Howard, Bursar? What about them? A colleague is ruined on the basis of incomplete evidence. Suddenly fresh evidence comes into your hands—new light may be shed, the whole truth of the affair may rest on this evidence—and you're too busy even to examine it carefully!

NIGHTINGALE

Too busy at that particular time. The moment the notebook arrived at the Bursary, I sent word to Skeffington. When he drew my attention to this page, naturally I examined it with the utmost care.

LEWIS

And by that time there was a blank space?

NIGHTINGALE

Yes.

LEWIS

I see. Bursar, after the cursory glance you gave this notebook—what did you do?

NIGHTINGALE

What did I do?

LEWIS

Yes. What did you do?

NIGHTINGALE

Put the notebook back with the others, of course.

LEWIS

You mean you put it back with the photograph still there?

NIGHTINGALE

(*Violently*)

Of course I mean that.

LEWIS

But the photograph had disappeared when the notebook was next opened?

NIGHTINGALE

That's what we've heard.

LEWIS

I'm sorry, have I misunderstood? The next person to look at the notebook was Skeffington, wasn't it?

NIGHTINGALE

So we've been told, so we've been told.

LEWIS

And when he looked at the notebook the photograph was missing?

NIGHTINGALE

Yes, yes, yes.

LEWIS

Then between the time that you closed the book and Skeffington opened it, the photograph had miraculously disappeared?

NIGHTINGALE

There was nothing miraculous about it.

LEWIS

Oh? Then perhaps you can tell us what happened?

NIGHTINGALE

Someone removed it, of course.

LEWIS

Who?

NIGHTINGALE
I've no idea.

LEWIS
Haven't you?

NIGHTINGALE
Why shouldn't one of Howard's friends have removed it—the perfectly genuine photograph—just to get this started again—not to
make any bones about it, just to point their fingers at me!

LEWIS
But supposing the photograph was not genuine? Supposing it was a
fake?

NIGHTINGALE
It wasn't.

LEWIS
You can't possibly know one way or the other. You only gave it a
cursory glance. —If a friend would remove a genuine photograph,
who would remove a fake, Bursar?

NIGHTINGALE
An enemy, of course.

LEWIS
Exactly.

NIGHTINGALE
What are you trying to make me say? Howard was a most unpopular man. He had dozens of enemies besides . . .

(*He stops.*)

LEWIS

Yes? Were you about to say besides *yourself?*

(*Pause*)

NIGHTINGALE

He made enemies right and left.

LEWIS

More right than left, surely.

(LEWIS *turns and puts the notebook back on the table in front of the Seniors.*)

You don't like Howard, do you, Bursar?

NIGHTINGALE

I have no personal animus against him.

LEWIS

But you have something else, haven't you? Something more insidious. You have political animus.

NIGHTINGALE

I don't approve of his political convictions, if that's what you mean.

LEWIS

I mean more than that.

(*With increasing force*)

Don't you believe that a man of Howard's convictions is a bad man? Don't you believe that a man of his convictions isn't to be trusted in any circumstances? Don't you believe that he's not a man of the same kind as yourself? Don't you believe that such men ought to be got rid of?

DAWSON-HILL
Really, Master, you can't permit—

NIGHTINGALE

(*Suddenly on his feet, blazing*)

All right! All right! I'll answer! Yes! I do believe he's not to be trusted! I do believe he's fundamentally different! I do believe he ought to be got rid of! We should never have elected such a man. Never, never, never!

LEWIS
Why? Because he believes what he believes? Because he thinks what he thinks?

NIGHTINGALE
Because he is *what* he is!

LEWIS

(*Triumphantly*)

Ah! Thank you, Bursar.

(*He sits down. A murmur from the Court.*)

(NIGHTINGALE *looks about him, flushed, defiant, confused. He turns to return to his seat on the Court.* DAWSON-HILL *rises.*)

DAWSON-HILL

(*Quietly*)

Just one moment, Doctor Nightingale.

(NIGHTINGALE *sits down again.*)

(DAWSON-HILL *crosses to the centre table, picks up the notebook and comes down to the witness chair.*)

DAWSON-HILL

Doctor Nightingale, I am bound to ask you this. Did you at any time remove or cause to be removed a photograph from this note-book?

NIGHTINGALE

I did not.

DAWSON-HILL

Do you believe that Professor Palairet faked any photograph at any time?

NIGHTINGALE

I do not.

DAWSON-HILL

You still believe that Howard is guilty?

NIGHTINGALE

(*Fiercely*)

As much as I have ever believed anything.

DAWSON-HILL

Thank you, Doctor Nightingale.

(NIGHTINGALE *returns to his seat on the Court. He stares out of a back window, isolated, apart.*)

CRAWFORD

Are there any further witnesses?

LEWIS

No, Master. I have here a statement from Doctor Skeffington which exactly corroborates all that the Court has heard from Sir Francis

Getliffe. I should like to present it in evidence but I do not propose
to call him.

(*He hands a document to* CRAWFORD.)

CRAWFORD
Does either Counsel wish to address the Court?

DAWSON-HILL
With the Court's permission. Master, four times the Court has been
concerned with this issue. You will not wish me to recapitulate the
evidence. Today, there has been one critical piece of testimony—
the speculations of Sir Francis Getliffe. I am sure my colleague will
agree with me—it is quite obviously incontrovertible—none of Sir
Francis's speculations is provable in law. Nevertheless I must warn
the Court that were it to reverse its decision, were it to reinstate
Howard, it would be giving weight to those speculations. Speculations which, by a fantastic stretch of improbability, might involve
the good name of a member of this Court. . . . Master, there has
been a piece of scientific fraud. The Court previously had to choose
between attributing this fraud to one of two men. One, a man rightly
honoured and respected, an eminent scholar, who cannot be present
to defend himself. The other, a man whom we can form our own
opinions of. Master, I do not possess the resources of my distinguished colleague. I don't find it easy to denigrate good men, or to
find virtues in those who have renounced all that most of us stand
for. Had I been a member of the Court, I should have made the same
choice the Court has made before. I now suggest to the Court that
in spite of the painful circumstances, all it can do is to repeat that
choice and reiterate that decision.

(*He sits down.*)

CRAWFORD
Eliot?

**LEWIS**

(*Rises*)

Master, like my colleague, I do not intend to recapitulate what the Court has heard so often. But with respect, I suggest to the Court that today it has heard not one, but two pieces of critical testimony —Sir Francis Getliffe's, and the Bursar's. The Bursar did not speculate. He made a categorical and quite uncompromising statement, not only that in his view Doctor Howard should never have been elected a Fellow of this College, but that, and I quote: "He ought to be got rid of." He gave his reasons—deeply felt, highly emotional reasons. Master, making up names for what we do not like and cannot bother to examine carefully is a common and dangerous pastime. We all know scientists whose politics are the same as Howard's, and whose integrity is absolute. And yet this Court has heard the view expressed—violently expressed by one of its own members—that character and belief go hand in hand. Isn't this nonsense, and dangerous nonsense?

(*With mounting force and passion*)

Isn't it the chronic danger, the madness of our time, for the world outside this College to divide into two halves? For each half to be blacked out and blinded by a fog of prejudice, so thick that people on the two sides are ceasing to think of each other as belonging to the same species? Hasn't this fog, this murderous, lunatic fog of prejudice, which is daily suffocating man's natural tolerance and understanding of his brother man, seeped inside these College walls and obscured this case from the beginning? Isn't *that* the heart and kernel, the *crux* of this whole affair? In the name of justice, in the name of tolerance, in the name of *survival*, I ask the Court to revoke its decision, and declare Howard innocent.

(*He sits down.*)

**CRAWFORD**

(*At length, quietly*)

Thank you, Eliot. Thank you, Dawson-Hill. And now, gentlemen, if you will withdraw, the Court will consider its finding. . . .

(LEWIS *and* DAWSON-HILL *rise, come to below the centre table and bow to the Court. As they turn to go out, the lights fade.*)

(*During the blackout the College bell is heard striking 7 times.*)

(*The lights are lowered to denote the passage of several hours. When they come up, it is late afternoon. The Seniors are seated as before:* WINSLOW, *his head sunk like an old eagle,* BROWN, *bolt upright,* NIGHTINGALE, *with his arms crossed over his chest,* CRAWFORD, *enigmatic, gazing in front of him.* LEWIS *and* DAWSON-HILL *come back into the room. They bow to the Court.*)

CRAWFORD

Be seated, gentlemen.

(LEWIS *and* DAWSON-HILL *return to their seats.*)

I apologise for keeping you so long, but we have had a little difficulty in expressing our intention.

(*Rings bell*)

However, we are, I think, ready now.

(*To* NEWBY, *who has entered*)

Ask Dr. Howard to come in, please.

NEWBY

Dr. Howard left some time ago, sir.

CRAWFORD

(*Taken aback*)

Left? You mean he left the immediate vicinity of the Combination Room, or left the College?

NEWBY

I couldn't say, sir. He's not outside. Mrs. Howard is here, sir. She, too, was asking for Dr. Howard.

CRAWFORD

Eliot, have you any knowledge of Howard's whereabouts?

LEWIS

No, Master. While the Court deliberated, I waited in my brother's rooms.

CRAWFORD

Well, I hardly think we can delay further. We shall have to proceed without him. Thank you, Newby.

(NEWBY *goes out.*)

Gentlemen, before we dispatch our business, there is one point I desire to stress with all possible force. . . .

(*Emphatically*)

In the course of the Court's deliberations, none of us has for one moment entertained the thought that any Fellow of this College—other than the man whom the Court originally deprived—could possibly have acted except with good intentions and according to the code of men devoted to science or other branches of learning. I hope that is clearly understood.

(WINSLOW *glances sideways at* NIGHTINGALE, *who stares straight ahead.*)

It remains for me now, as Master of the College and President of the Court of Seniors, to formulate our finding. . . .

"March 20th, 1961. At a meeting of the Court of Seniors held this day, present: The Master, Mr. Winslow, Mr. Brown, Dr. Nightingale, it was resolved as follows: that the testimony was not sufficient to support the Order for the Deprivation of D. C. Howard, dated October 17th, 1959, and that the Order for such deprivation is hereby quashed.

(*Pause*)

It was further resolved that Dr. Howard's Fellowship should be presumed to have continued without interruption during the period of deprivation and that his Fellowship shall continue until it lapses by the effluxion of time. The order is signed by the Master, Mr. Winslow, *and* Mr. Brown."

(BROWN *gives brief nod of understanding to* LEWIS.)

Dr. Nightingale, Bursar of the College and Secretary of the Court of Seniors, wishes to have his dissent to the above recorded. The Order is sealed with the College seal.

(*He puts down the paper.*)

Is that acceptable to you, Dawson-Hill?

DAWSON-HILL
I don't pretend to be entirely happy, Master.

CRAWFORD
If you have anything further to say—?

DAWSON-HILL
Would that be the slightest use?

CRAWFORD
Eliot?

(*Pause*)

LEWIS
I am satisfied, Master.

CRAWFORD

(*With relief*)

Then there the matter rests. I seem to recall making an earlier observation to the effect that sensible men usually reach sensible conclusions.

(*Rings his bell*)

I think I may add that on this occasion such has proved to be the case.

(NEWBY *enters.* CRAWFORD *hands him the order.*)

Will you please affix this to the notice-board?

NEWBY
Yes, sir.

BROWN
Just a minute, Newby.

(BROWN *whispers something to* CRAWFORD.)

CRAWFORD
Ah, indeed. By all means. Newby, is Mrs. Howard still outside?

NEWBY
Yes, sir.

CRAWFORD

(*Handing him another sheet*)

Kindly give her this copy for her husband.

NEWBY
Right, sir.

(*He goes out.*)

CRAWFORD
Gentlemen, the Court is adjourned *sine die.*

(*All rise.*)

Eliot—Dawson-Hill—if you care to join us in the Lodge for a glass of Marsala, you will be more than welcome.

(*To the others, as they go*)

I think that all went off quite smoothly, don't you?

(*Followed by* WINSLOW, BROWN, *and* NIGHTINGALE, CRAWFORD *passes into the Lodge.*)

LEWIS

(*As* NIGHTINGALE *reaches the door*)

Bursar.

(NIGHTINGALE *turns.*)

I hope you won't feel that anything I have said today leaves you no alternative—I hope you won't resign, Alec.

NIGHTINGALE

(*Steadily*)

To live here now will not be easy. You've put me in a false position. But I have always fought for my beliefs—and to surrender my post to another, possibly weaker man would be to give up the fight. I do not believe in surrender—any more than I believe in compromise. No, I shall not resign.

(*He turns and goes out the other way.*)

LEWIS

Inflexible to the finish.

DAWSON-HILL

(*Relaxed—the Barrister after the battle*)

One can't altogether blame him, you know.

(*Offering* LEWIS *a cigarette and taking one himself*)

After all, it's quite possible he's as blameless as Howard.

LEWIS

(*A statement—not a question*)

You believe that.

DAWSON-HILL

Don't you?

LEWIS

I don't know, Gilbert. I don't know.

DAWSON-HILL

My dear chap, you know as well as I do that infernal print could just as easily have fallen out as been torn out. More than likely, I'd say. From the look of his notebook Palairet wasn't much of a hand with his cellotape. No, there's not a shadow of proof against Nightingale—or against Palairet, or against Howard. There's no *proof* against anyone.

LEWIS

(*Troubled*)

You set out to get a wrong righted—and end up with the finite chance of having wronged two other people.

DAWSON-HILL

Still searching for absolute justice? There's no such lady. Never mind, you're the man of the hour. I must say, you played it very neatly, very neatly indeed. The moment I saw old Brown's eyebrows twitching, I knew I was done for.

LEWIS

(*With a smile*)

Yes, so did I.

(LAURA *enters, holding the Order in hand.* DAWSON-HILL *collects his papers and turns to* LEWIS.)

DAWSON-HILL

Lewis, I'll see you in the Lodge.

(LEWIS *nods and* DAWSON-HILL *exits to Lodge.*)

LAURA

(*Quietly*)

Who wrote this?

LEWIS

It was the joint effort of the Court. I believe it gave them some difficulty.

LAURA

(*Carefully*)

"Fellowship presumed to have continued until it lapses by the effluxion of time." Do you know *when* Don's Fellowship lapses? September the fourth. It's March already. They're taking him back and kicking him out in the same breath. He's lost a year and a half. We want that year and a half back.

LEWIS

(*Patiently*)

Look, Mrs. Howard, this gives you everything essential. Your husband's name is cleared. He won't have a black mark against him.

His Fellowship will run its course. I don't say it's generous—but you've got the substance of what you wanted.

LAURA

Half a loaf. Oh no, thank you. We're not going to be fobbed off with that. I can't understand how you could let them give us a slap in the face like this.

LEWIS

Do you think it was easy to get this much?

LAURA

I know your kind. You played it safe. Of course, they're your friends, aren't they? I don't like the Establishment, but I'm beginning to think the real menace is the Establishment behind the Establishment, and that's what you're a specialist in!

LEWIS

(*Grimly*)

Now listen for once. I haven't done much, but without me I doubt if you'd have got any satisfaction at all. Without Francis Getliffe, I know you wouldn't. It may cost him the Mastership and my brother promotion and Skeffington his job. We've done our piece. And that's enough.

LAURA

(*Strongly*)

And you call that justice? This filthy compromise?

LEWIS

(*With equal strength*)

Sometimes there *is* no slick solution. Sometimes the only hope is for one side to meet the other halfway. Sometimes all you have left is compromise.

LAURA

(*Blazing*)

There's one thing you always have left. You can fight.

(HOWARD *appears in the doorway. Neither of them notice him.*)

LEWIS

(*Suddenly utterly weary*)

Yes, you can fight. Fight, fight—you can fight to the death. Lord knows there are fools enough on the other side ready and waiting to fight you back. And what happens to the rest of us, caught in the cross fire of your total madness?

(*Passionately*)

Christ, isn't there somewhere a solitary sentient human being humble enough and clear enough to stand up and say, "in the name of sanity—in the name of sheer, flat common sense—let's *stop!*"

(HOWARD *comes slowly in.*)

LAURA

What happened? Don? What happened? Where have you been?

HOWARD

Walking. Down by the Backs.

LAURA

I was worried. You might have left a message.

HOWARD

I'm sorry. I wanted to be alone.


LEWIS

You've seen the Order?


HOWARD

Yes. I'm glad.


LAURA

Glad? You're glad?


HOWARD

They seem to have decided I'm not a liar.


LAURA

That's nothing. We're not settling for—


HOWARD

It's enough.


LAURA

Don, leave this to me—


HOWARD

No! I'm fed up with being talked about. I'm not going to be talked about any more by anyone. You understand?


LAURA

Don, listen to me—

HOWARD

(*Violently*)

No! Laura! For God's sake—will you let me *breathe?*

(*He moves up to the windows. She stares at him.* NEWBY *enters from the hall.*)

NEWBY

(*To* HOWARD)

Excuse me, Doctor Howard, sir.

HOWARD

Yes?

NEWBY

You were asking for Dr. Skeffington. He's just coming out of the library, sir.

HOWARD

Oh, right. Thank you, Newby.

(NEWBY *goes.*)

LAURA

(*Astonished*)

Skeffington? What could *you* possibly have to say to Skeffington?

HOWARD

I don't know. I've never tried. I thought of starting with "thanks." And then there's the weather . . . and life and death . . . and what are we here for? . . . And then there are one or two things *he* might like to ask *me*. This may take quite a time. So don't wait if you don't want to.

(*Deliberately, as he leaves*)

Don't wait.

(LAURA *stares after him, stunned.*)

LAURA

(*At length*)

Stupid of me . . . I should have known . . . I should have known, if he won, I'd lose him. Stupid . . .

LEWIS

Aren't you reading more into a gesture—

LAURA

(*Calmly, without self-pity*)

No. He's gone. I know the pattern. . . .

LEWIS

Go with him.

(*Pause*)

LAURA

No. Middle roads are not for me. I'll fight for my world and win— or go under.

(*With complete assurance*)

But I shan't go under. I shall be here.

LEWIS

(*With reluctant admiration*)

Yes . . . Yes, I believe you will. Whoever goes under, you'll go on. You're a natural survivor. Come the Flood, there you'll be—right on the top of Ararat—organising the drainage.

LAURA

You don't have to comfort me.

LEWIS

I'm not. I'm comforting myself. . .

LAURA

Good-bye.

(*She turns and goes.* LEWIS *stares after her.* DAWSON-HILL *enters from the Lodge and crosses to* LEWIS.)

DAWSON-HILL

Lewis, the Master's waiting to drink your health. Aren't you coming? Lewis?

LEWIS

Yes, yes, I'm coming.

DAWSON-HILL

Don't look so troubled, my dear chap. You won. What more do you want—peace of mind?

(*He leaves* LEWIS *standing thoughtfully in the centre of the stage and goes quietly back into the Lodge.* LEWIS *smiles enigmatically, then turns and goes quickly after* DAWSON-HILL *as—*)

## THE CURTAIN FALLS.